ACCUPLACER
Mathematics Exam
Workbook

SECRETS

Study Guide
Your Key to Exam Success

ACCUPLACER Test Practice Questions &
Review for the ACCUPLACER Exam

Dear Future Exam Success Story:

Congratulations on your purchase of our study guide. Our goal in writing our study guide was to cover the content on the test, as well as provide insight into typical test taking mistakes and how to overcome them.

Standardized tests are a key component of being successful, which only increases the importance of doing well in the high-pressure high-stakes environment of test day. How well you do on this test will have a significant impact on your future, and we have the research and practical advice to help you execute on test day.

The product you're reading now is designed to exploit weaknesses in the test itself, and help you avoid the most common errors test takers frequently make.

How to use this study guide

We don't want to waste your time. Our study guide is fast-paced and fluff-free. We suggest going through it a number of times, as repetition is an important part of learning new information and concepts.

First, read through the study guide completely to get a feel for the content and organization. Read the general success strategies first, and then proceed to the content sections. Each tip has been carefully selected for its effectiveness.

Second, read through the study guide again, and take notes in the margins and highlight those sections where you may have a particular weakness.

Finally, bring the manual with you on test day and study it before the exam begins.

Your success is our success

We would be delighted to hear about your success. Send us an email and tell us your story. Thanks for your business and we wish you continued success.

Sincerely,

Mometrix Test Preparation Team

Need more help? Check out our flashcards at:
http://MometrixFlashcards.com/ACCUPLACER

TABLE OF CONTENTS

Top 20 Test Taking Tips

1. Carefully follow all the test registration procedures
2. Know the test directions, duration, topics, question types, how many questions
3. Setup a flexible study schedule at least 3-4 weeks before test day
4. Study during the time of day you are most alert, relaxed, and stress free
5. Maximize your learning style; visual learner use visual study aids, auditory learner use auditory study aids
6. Focus on your weakest knowledge base
7. Find a study partner to review with and help clarify questions
8. Practice, practice, practice
9. Get a good night's sleep; don't try to cram the night before the test
10. Eat a well balanced meal
11. Know the exact physical location of the testing site; drive the route to the site prior to test day
12. Bring a set of ear plugs; the testing center could be noisy
13. Wear comfortable, loose fitting, layered clothing to the testing center; prepare for it to be either cold or hot during the test
14. Bring at least 2 current forms of ID to the testing center
15. Arrive to the test early; be prepared to wait and be patient
16. Eliminate the obviously wrong answer choices, then guess the first remaining choice
17. Pace yourself; don't rush, but keep working and move on if you get stuck
18. Maintain a positive attitude even if the test is going poorly
19. Keep your first answer unless you are positive it is wrong
20. Check your work, don't make a careless mistake

Arithmetic

Computations with Integers and Fractions

This section measures your ability to correctly perform mathematical operations involving integers (positive and negative whole numbers and zero) and fractions (which may be either negative or positive.) The mathematical operations used in these problems include addition, subtraction, multiplication, and division. As a result, you must be comfortable performing these four operations when they involve negative and positive numbers.

Two positive integers can be added using simple rules of addition and will always yield a positive result. Add two negative integers together as if they were positive and then change the sign of the answer to negative. When one integer is positive and the other is negative, take the number with the smaller absolute value and subtract it from the larger. Next, change the sign of the answer to be the same as the sign of the number with the larger absolute value.

> For example, to add 5 and –7, subtract 7 – 5 and then change the sign of the answer to a negative sign since 7 is greater than 5 and –7 is negative:
>
> $$5 + (-7) = -2$$

Subtracting one integer from another can be solved by changing the problem to an addition problem and using the rules for addition. First, change the operator from subtraction to addition. Next, reverse the sign of the second integer. Last, add the integers together.

> For example, to calculate –5 – 2, change it to addition and then follow the rules for addition:
>
> $$-5 - 2 = -5 + (-2)$$
> $$= -7$$

When multiplying or dividing two integers, perform the operation as if the numbers were both positive and then change the sign of the answer as follows: If the two integers have the same sign, then their product is positive; if they have different signs, then their product is negative. In addition to the rules above, special steps must be taken when dealing with fractions. One rule of fractions is that if you multiply or divide the numerator and denominator of a fraction by the same number, the result is an equivalent fraction (i.e. the fractions are equal to one another.)

For example, $\frac{1}{2}$ and $\frac{3}{6}$ are equivalent fractions because if you multiply the numerator and denominator of $\frac{1}{2}$ by 3, the result is $\frac{3}{6}$:

$$\frac{1}{2} \times \frac{3}{3} = \frac{3}{6}$$

When adding or subtracting fractions, first find a common denominator to both fractions. The best choice is a number called the lowest common denominator (LCD), which is the smallest number for which both denominators are factors. Once you find this value, rewrite each fraction as an equivalent fraction whose denominator is their LCD. Then add or subtract the numerators and put the answer over the LCD.

For instance, to add $-\frac{1}{6}$ and $\frac{5}{9}$, first rewrite them with the LCD of 6 and 9, which is 18:

$$-\frac{1}{6} \times \frac{3}{3} = -\frac{3}{18}$$

$$\frac{5}{9} \times \frac{2}{2} = \frac{10}{18}$$

Then add the numerators and put the result over 18.

$$-\frac{1}{6} + \frac{5}{9} = -\frac{3}{18} + \frac{10}{18}$$

$$= \frac{-3+10}{18}$$

$$= \frac{7}{18}$$

Similarly, to compare two fractions (i.e. determine which is greater) or put a list of fractions in order, rewrite them so that they have the same denominator and order them based on the numerators.

There are an infinite number of equivalent ways to write any fraction. The best choice is to express fractions in their lowest (or simplest) terms. A fraction is in lowest terms when its numerator and denominator do not have a common factor greater than 1. If a fraction is not in lowest terms, divide the numerator and denominator by their greatest common factor (GCF.) The GCF is the largest number that is a factor of both the numerator and denominator. For example, the fraction $\frac{4}{12}$ is not in lowest terms, because both 4 and 12 share a GCF of 4, and thus can be rewritten as $\frac{1}{3}$.

Multiplying fractions does not require finding a common denominator. Simply multiply the numerators together to create the new numerator, and multiply the denominators together to create the new denominator. It is a good practice to make sure that both fractions are first written in lowest terms, and factors common between the numerator of one fraction and the denominator of the other are cancelled out, to simplify the multiplication. Always express the final result in lowest terms.

Dividing two fractions is done by changing the problem to a multiplication problem and then using the rules for multiplication. First, change the operation to multiplication. Next, invert (or flip) the numerator and denominator of the second fraction.

For example, divide $\frac{2}{3}$ by $\frac{4}{5}$ as shown below. Note that $\frac{2}{3}$ and $\frac{5}{4}$ can be reduced prior to multiplication by cancelling out a factor of 2 in both the numerator and denominator:

$$\frac{2}{3} \div \frac{4}{5} = \frac{2}{3} \times \frac{5}{4}$$

$$= \frac{1}{3} \times \frac{5}{2}$$

$$= \frac{5}{6}$$

Some of the problems in this section involve more than one operation. Consequently, students must understand how to follow the order of operations to answer the questions correctly. A helpful mnemonic for the order of operations is "PEMDAS," which stands for "Parentheses, Exponents, Multiplication, Division, Addition, Subtraction." If a problem involves many different operations, first calculate the values inside parentheses, then compute the value of exponential expressions, then perform any multiplication, then division, and lastly addition and subtraction. Always remember to simplify fractions before working with them in expressions.

Computations with Integers and Fractions Questions

1. $5(3 - 9) \div 3 =$
   a. -10
   b. 2
   c. 5
   d. 20

2. $\frac{4 - (-12)}{-9 + 5} =$
   a. -8
   b. -4
   c. -2
   d. 4

3. $4\left(-\frac{1}{2} + \frac{3}{5}\right) =$

   a. $\frac{2}{5}$

   b. $\frac{4}{5}$

   c. 1

   d. $\frac{6}{5}$

4. Order $\frac{7}{15}, \frac{9}{20}, \frac{2}{5}$, and $\frac{13}{30}$ from least to greatest.

   a. $\frac{2}{5}, \frac{9}{20}, \frac{13}{30}, \frac{7}{15}$

   b. $\frac{2}{5}, \frac{13}{30}, \frac{9}{20}, \frac{7}{15}$

   c. $\frac{9}{20}, \frac{2}{5}, \frac{13}{30}, \frac{7}{15}$

   d. $\frac{13}{30}, \frac{2}{5}, \frac{9}{20}, \frac{7}{15}$

5. $\frac{3}{8} \div \frac{6}{11} =$

   a. $\frac{9}{44}$

   b. $\frac{15}{88}$

   c. $\frac{11}{16}$

   d. $\frac{33}{56}$

Computation with Decimal Numbers

This section measures your ability to correctly perform mathematical operation involving decimal numbers. Decimal numbers are numbers with at least one digit after the decimal point. The digits after the decimal point (called the number's decimal places) represent quantities less than one. The first place to the right of the decimal point is called the tenths place, the second place is called the hundredths place, the third is called the thousandths place, and so on. Any decimal can be quickly converted to a fraction (though a potentially unwieldy one) as in the example below:

$$5.8139 = 5 + \frac{8}{10} + \frac{1}{100} + \frac{3}{1000} + \frac{9}{10,000}$$

$$= \frac{58,139}{10,000}$$

The mathematical operations used in the problems in this section include addition, subtraction, multiplication, and division. As a result, students must be comfortable performing these four operations when they involve decimal numbers.

Add and subtract decimal numbers by first aligning the two numbers vertically, making sure that the decimal points are lined up one under the other. This will ensure that all corresponding decimal places (the tenths place, the hundredths place, etc.) are lined up as well. If one number has less decimal places than the other, add trailing zeroes until the number of decimal places are equal (3.2 is equal to 3.20.) Then add (or subtract) the corresponding decimal places starting from the right and working to the left, and bring down the decimal point at the end.

For example, to subtract 1.458 from 3.2:

$$
\begin{array}{r}
3.2 \\
- 1.458 \\
\hline
\end{array}
$$

$$
\begin{array}{r}
3.200 \\
- 1.458 \\
\hline
1.742
\end{array}
$$

Multiply two decimal numbers as if they were large integers, again arranging them vertically and adding trailing zeroes for the number with less decimal places. After all numbers have been multiplied and added together, apply the decimal point to this result. This can be determined by counting the number of decimal places in each factor and adding them together. This will be the number of decimal places in the product, applied by counting places moving right to left.

Division of two decimal numbers is performed like long division on integers, with adjustments for the decimals. If the divisor is a decimal number, move the decimal to the right until no decimal places remain. Next, move the decimal place for the dividend the same number of places (adding zeroes if necessary to the end of the number.) Then complete the long division.

Finally, the questions in this section will cover rounding numbers to a given decimal place (e.g. to the nearest whole number, or to the nearest hundredth.) Decimals can be rounded by locating the decimal place to round to, and assessing the number to the right of that digit. If the number is below 5, the decimal will be rounded down. For example, rounding 2.54 to the tenths place yields 2.5 (the 4 rounds down to 0.) If the number is at or above 5, the decimal will be rounded up. For example, rounding 2.938 to the nearest hundredth yields 2.94 (the 3 rounds up to 4 because of the 8.)

Computation with Decimal Numbers Questions

1. $8.31 + 6.7 + 1.889 =$
    a. 15.899
    b. 16.89
    c. 16.899
    d. 17.89

2. $12.94 \times 5.8 =$
    a. 64.952
    b. 75.052
    c. 649.52
    d. 750.52

3. Round 94.542 to the nearest tenth.
    a. 94.5
    b. 94.55
    c. 94.6
    d. 95

4. $(45.7 - 58.2) \times 0 \times (4.69 \div 1.34) =$
    a. −68
    b. −55.5
    c. 0
    d. 68

5. $14.32 - 12.915 =$
    a. 1.405
    b. 1.414
    c. 2.17
    d. 2.405

Problems involving Percents

This section covers problems involving percents. A "percent" is some number out of 100. For example, 85% (read "eighty-five percent") means 85 out of 100, which is equivalent to the fraction $\frac{85}{100}$. Percents can be expressed as any positive number, including decimals, fractions, and values larger than 100. The five numbers shown below are all examples of percents:

$$1,589\% \qquad \frac{3}{5}\% \qquad \frac{97}{100}\% \qquad 0.8\% \qquad 519.2301\%$$

To answer the questions in this section correctly, students must understand what "percent" means, how to identify a percent, and also how to convert percents to fractions or decimal numbers.

A percent can be converted to a fraction by placing the number over 100 as shown above. While the result is a fraction that is equal to the original percent, it may not be expressed in lowest terms. Put it in lowest terms by dividing the numerator and denominator by their greatest common factor (GCF.)

For example, you can use this process to write 85% as a fraction in lowest terms:

$$85\% = \frac{85}{100}$$

$$= \frac{17}{20}$$

The reverse process can be used to convert a fraction to a percent. If the denominator is 100, convert it to a percent by removing the denominator and adding a percent sign (%) to the numerator. If the denominator is not 100, convert the fraction first to a decimal by dividing the numerator by the denominator. The decimal can be converted to a percent by multiplying it by 100, or equivalently, moving the decimal point two places to the right and then adding a percent sign (%.)

A percent can be converted to a decimal by dividing the percent value by 100 and removing the percent sign (%), or equivalently, move the decimal two places to the left. For example, the percent 52.48% and the decimal 0.5248 are equal.

This section also contains problems that require calculation of value given a percent.

For example, calculate 40% of 62. The word "of" means multiplication, so to find 40% of 62, write it as a multiplication problem:

$$40\% \times 62$$

Then calculate the product by converting 40% to either a fraction or decimal and multiplying the two numbers together:

$$40\% \times 62 = 0.4 \times 62$$
$$= 24.8$$

Thus, 40% of 62 is 24.8.

This section also contains problems that require calculation of a percentage from a given value, such as "What percent of 40 is 35?" or equivalently, "35 is what percent of 40?" The easiest way to solve problems like this is to think of a percent as a part divided by the whole (i.e. $\frac{\text{part}}{\text{whole}}$). The example above states that 35 is some percent of 40, or "35 parts out of 40." Therefore, in terms of the fraction $\frac{\text{part}}{\text{whole}}$, the part is 35 and the whole is 40. Plug these values into this fraction, divide, and then convert the decimal to a percentage as shown below:

$$\frac{\text{part}}{\text{whole}} = \frac{35}{40}$$
$$= 0.875$$
$$= 87.5\%$$

Problems involving Percents Questions

1. What is 56% of 25?
   - a. 10
   - b. 11
   - c. 12
   - d. 14

2. Write 45% as a fraction in lowest terms.
   - a. $\frac{2}{5}$
   - b. $\frac{9}{20}$
   - c. $\frac{4}{5}$
   - d. $\frac{20}{9}$

3. What percent of 56 is 42?
   - a. 60%
   - b. 72.5%
   - c. 75%
   - d. 85%

4. A school has 48 boys and 72 girls. What percent of the students are boys?
   - a. 30%
   - b. 35%
   - c. 40%
   - d. 45%

5. What is $\frac{1}{2}$% of 40?
   - a. 0.2
   - b. 2
   - c. 8
   - d. 20

Estimation, Ordering, Number Sense

This section covers how to correctly estimate numbers, put numbers in order from least to greatest, and use mathematical intuition to quickly and accurately solve problems. When solving problems using arithmetic, it is good idea to have a ballpark estimate of the answer. That way, if an answer is much larger or smaller than the estimate, a re-check of the work can be done to see if there was a mistake.

Estimation means approximating the result of a mathematical operation. Because it involves an approximation, estimation is a lot like rounding but extends this idea to include mathematical operations like addition, multiplication, exponents, and square roots, rather than just single numbers. In general, estimating mathematical expressions saves time. Although an estimated answer will not be exact, it can be found much more quickly than an exact answer.

To estimate the sum or difference of two numbers, first round the numbers to a reasonable place (the larger the rounding place, the less accurate the result.) All numbers should be rounded to the same decimal place even if it seems inappropriate for some of them. Next, add or subtract the result.

> For example, to add 578,239 and 89,198, round them to the nearest hundred thousand and then add the result.
>
> $$578{,}239 + 89{,}198 \approx 600{,}000 + 100{,}000$$
> $$\approx 700{,}000$$

To estimate the product or quotient of two numbers, round each number to their first significant decimal place. In other words, round each number to the first decimal place that is not a zero. Then multiply or divide the rounded numbers.

> For example:
>
> $$5093 \times 73 \approx 5000 \times 70$$
> $$\approx 350{,}000$$

This process exploits the fact that multiplying and dividing by powers of 10 is relatively easy in the decimal system. For instance, to multiply two very large numbers with lots of trailing zeroes (trailing zeroes are zeroes at the end of a number), multiply the parts that aren't zeroes and then add in all the trailing zeroes at the end.

Estimating the square root of a number is done by finding its nearest perfect square. A perfect square is a positive integer that can be written as the square of another number. For instance, 16 and 100 are both perfect squares since $4^2 = 16$ and $10^2 = 100$. The square root of a perfect square is always a whole number. To estimate the square root of a number, round the original number to its nearest perfect square and then take the square root of that value.

Questions in this section will also require that lists of different types of numbers be placed in order from least to greatest. First, convert all the numbers to the same format (fractions, decimals, percents with the same denominator, etc.) if this not already the case. Next, arrange the numbers in order. If they are all decimals, compare the digits in like decimal place starting with leftmost place and working toward the right. Note that negative numbers are smaller than positive numbers and if the absolute value of a negative number is greater than the absolute value of another negative number, then the first one is smaller than the second. For example, -56 is smaller than -12 because $56 > 12$ and 56 is further away on the number line from zero.

Number sense is the phrase used for a person's intuition for numbers and magnitudes. It involves a wide range of concepts, including estimation, rounding, ordering, comparison, and measurement. Consequently, there is no one set of instructions that can be used for all questions involving number sense.

Estimation, Ordering, Number Sense Questions

1. Estimate the square root of 82.
   a. 7
   b. 8
   c. 9
   d. 10

2. Estimate $80{,}389 \times 597.39$.
   a. 400,000
   b. 4,800,000
   c. 40,000,000
   d. 48,000,000

3. Order 1.71, $\frac{8}{5}$, -2, and 1.685 from least to greatest.

   a. $-2, \frac{8}{5}, 1.685, 1.71$

   b. $-2, 1.685, \frac{8}{5}, 1.71$

   c. $1.685, \frac{8}{5}, 1.71, -2$

   d. $\frac{8}{5}, 1.685, 1.71, -2$

4. Which of the following is closest to the sum of $\frac{47}{45}$ and $\frac{20}{21}$?

   a. $\frac{436}{315}$

   b. 1.53

   c. 2

   d. 4

5. Which of the following is the greatest?
   a. 24.1% of 120
   b. 34.2% of 99
   c. 49.4% of 72
   d. 51.1% of 90

Word Problems and Applications

This section covers the usage of arithmetic skills to solve word problems. To be successful in this section, you must be able to correctly interpret information given to you in words and apply the various skills of arithmetic, including performing calculations with integers, fractions, percents and decimal numbers, estimating the result of a calculation, and using number sense.

Word problems ask questions about real-life situations. The first step in solving a word problem is to interpret the information given in the problem and formulate a plan to answer the question. This will almost certainly involve performing at least one calculation using numbers in the text, and possibly multiple calculations will be needed to solve the problem.

It is a good idea to carefully reread the problem at the end to make sure the expression created to solve the word problem is accurate and complete.

Word Problems and Applications Questions

1. A school has 300 students, and three-fifths of the students are girls. How many girls attend the school?
    a. 140 girls
    b. 150 girls
    c. 180 girls
    d. 200 girls

2. Jerry goes to the grocery store and pays $2.55 for milk, $3.79 for oranges, and $3.09 for eggs. If he gives the cashier a $20 bill, what will his change be?
    a. $10.57
    b. $10.72
    c. $11.27
    d. $11.62

3. Nancy pays 5% sales tax on a car that costs $25,000. What is the cost of the car including sales tax?
    a. $26,250
    b. $26,800
    c. $27,200
    d. $28,000

4. A school has 270 boys and 450 girls. What percentage of the student body are boys?
    a. 25%
    b. 37.5%
    c. 42.5%
    d. 60%

5. A company sold 810,602 computers last year for $895 each. How much was the total revenue for the computers, approximately?
    a. $56 million
    b. $72 million
    c. $560 million
    d. $720 million

Elementary Algebra

Real Numbers

This section measures your ability to correctly identify and manipulate real numbers. Any number that can be represented by a decimal number (including those with an infinite number of digits after the decimal point) is a real number. Visually, you can think of the real numbers as those numbers that can be represented by a point on a number line extending infinitely in both directions from zero.

Numbers that are not real are known as imaginary numbers. These numbers are rarely used in everyday math. They are typically found in higher level scientific applications, such as quantum mechanics. Imaginary numbers are real numbers multiplied by the imaginary unit, represented with the symbol i, such as $5i$, and are not covered in this workbook.

The set of real numbers is divided into two groups, rational numbers and irrational numbers. A rational numbers is a number that can be written as a fraction. Here, the word *rational* comes from the fact that the number can be written as the *ratio* of two integers. Included in this set are integers, fractions, and mixed numbers. In addition, two types of decimal numbers are also rational: those that terminate, and those that repeat. Terminating decimals are rational decimal numbers that eventually terminate or end, and repeating decimals are rational decimal numbers that repeat indefinitely. The five numbers below are all examples of rational numbers because they can all be written as fractions:

$$\frac{100}{3} \qquad -5 \qquad 11\frac{4}{9} \qquad 43.913 \qquad -0.9155155155\ldots$$

Irrational numbers, on the other hand, are real numbers that cannot be written as a fraction. Some examples of irrational numbers are square root radicals (which are discussed below) and often-used constants like π (the Greek letter "pi") and e. In fact, any non-terminating, non-repeating decimal is an irrational number.

This section includes problems that involve addition, subtraction, multiplication, and division of real numbers. As a result, students must be comfortable performing these four operations using the correct order of operations. Students should already be familiar with calculations involving fractions and decimal numbers from arithmetic, but they may be less familiar with calculations involving square root radicals.

A square root radical is a number such as $\sqrt{5}$, in other words, one that contains the radical sign ($\sqrt{}$). The number under the radical sign is called the radicand of the number. Additionally, some square root radicals have a coefficient, which is a number before the radical sign that is multiplied by the radical. For example, in $4\sqrt{7}$, 4 is a coefficient of the radical. If a coefficient is not shown on a radical, the coefficient is assumed to be 1 since one times any number is the number itself. Square root radicals can be added or subtracted through a process called combining "like" radicals. Like radicals are radicals with the same radicand, for example, $2\sqrt{3}$ and $\sqrt{3}$. To combine like radicals, add or subtract their coefficients and keep the radicand the same:

$$2\sqrt{3} + \sqrt{3} = 2\sqrt{3} + 1\sqrt{3}$$
$$= 3\sqrt{3}$$

On the other hand, square root radicals can be multiplied or divided, even if they are not like radicals. Multiply or divide the coefficients (if there are any) and then do the same for the radicands:

$$3\sqrt{5} \times 2\sqrt{11} = 6\sqrt{55}$$

In this example, the result cannot be simplified. But, in some cases, the product or quotient of two radicals may be simplified further.

To simplify a square root radical, check to see if the radicand is a perfect square. A perfect square is a positive integer that is the square of an integer, so numbers like 16 and 100 are perfect squares because $4^2 = 16$ and $10^2 = 100$. If the radicand of a square root radical is a perfect square, simplify by taking its square root.

If the radicand is not a perfect square, rewrite the radicand as the product of two numbers, the greatest perfect square factor (if one exists) and another factor.

For instance, simplify $\sqrt{45}$ by factoring 9, a perfect square factor, and 5:

$$\sqrt{45} = \sqrt{9 \times 5}$$

Next separate the result into two radicals using these factors:

$$\sqrt{9 \times 5} = \sqrt{9} \times \sqrt{5}$$

Finally, take the square root of the first factor. The result will be a square root radical with a coefficient.

$$\sqrt{9} \times \sqrt{5} = 3\sqrt{5}$$

Real Numbers Questions

1. Which of the following numbers is an irrational number?
   a. -5
   b. $-\frac{11}{8}$
   c. $0.\overline{33}$
   d. π

2. $\left(\frac{2}{3}-\frac{1}{4}\right) \div \frac{1}{4} =$
   a. $\frac{5}{48}$

   b. $\frac{1}{3}$

   c. $\frac{5}{3}$

   d. 48

3. $\frac{4.8-12.3}{-1-4} =$
   a. -2.5
   b. -1.5
   c. 1.5
   d. 2.5

4. $\sqrt{63} =$
   a. $3\sqrt{7}$
   b. $7\sqrt{3}$
   c. $7\sqrt{9}$
   d. $9\sqrt{7}$

5. $\sqrt{3} \times \sqrt{7} =$
   a. 3
   b. $\sqrt{21}$
   c. 10
   d. 21

Linear Equations, Inequalities and Systems

This section measures the ability to correctly solve linear equations, linear inequalities, and systems of linear equations. Here, the word *linear* refers to the fact that the equations can be graphically represented with a line. Symbolically, a linear equation is an equation of degree 1, and thus an equation whose highest degree is 1. The degree of a monomial is defined as the sum of the exponents of each of its variables. For example, the degree of $4a^3b^6$ is 9 because $3 + 6 = 9$. Therefore, a linear equation is an equation in which every monomial either has degree 0 (i.e. a constant) or degree 1 (i.e. a term with one variable whose exponent is 1.)

The solution to a linear equation is the number that satisfies the equation. In other words, if you substitute the solution for all occurrences of the variable in the equation, the result will be a true equality. For instance, $x = 5$ is the solution to the equation $x + 2 = 7$ because substitution of 5 for x results in a true equality, $5 + 2 = 7$. Generally speaking, a linear equation with one variable will have one and only one solution.

Two equations are considered equivalent if they have the same solution. For example, the equations, $4x = 12$ and $x - 1 = 2$, are equivalent because they both have the solution $x = 3$. Writing a series of equivalent equations can produce a solution for any linear equation. Start with a given equation, then using the basic rules of algebra, transform it through a series of equivalent equation until you finally reach an equation of the form *variable = number* (or vice versa). This number is the solution to the original equation.

Equations can be transformed using any of the rules for manipulating expressions, including distributing over parentheses; performing calculations with integers, fractions, decimals, and radicals; combining like terms; simplifying exponents; and so on. Notice that these rules only apply to expressions and thus can only be used to affect terms on one side of the equals sign. Consequently, they are of no use if you want to make changes to both sides of the equation.

However, any operation can be applied to one side of the equation as long as the same operation is applied to the other side as well.

For example, to solve the equation $3c = 6$, both sides can be divided by 3 and then simplified:

$$3c = 6$$

$$\frac{3c}{3} = \frac{6}{3}$$

$$c = 2$$

Some operations do not follow this rule (e.g. squaring both sides of an equation), but do not apply when solving linear equations.

To solve a linear equation with one variable, first simplify both sides of the equation.

For example, to solve the equation $3(x + 2) = 0$, first distribute the 3 on the left side:

$$3(x + 2) = 0$$

$$3x + 6 = 0$$

After both sides are simplified, isolate the variable on one side of the equation. A variable is said to be isolated if it appears alone (save for a coefficient) on one side of the equation and does not appear at all on the other side. Any term can be "moved" from one side of the equation to the other by subtracting it from both sides, or equivalently, by adding its opposite. In the example above, the term $3x$ is isolated by subtracting 6 from both sides:

$$3x + 6 = 0$$

$$(3x + 6) - 6 = 0 - 6$$

$$3x = -6$$

The resulting equation can be solved for x by dividing both sides by the coefficient of the variable term, which is 3:

- 22 -

$$3x = -6$$

$$\frac{3x}{3} = \frac{-6}{3}$$

$$x = -2$$

Always validate a solution by substituting the value back into the original equation and confirming that it satisfies the equation. For the example above, substitute -2 for x into the original equation:

$$3(x + 2) = 0$$

$$3[(-2) + 2] = 0$$

$$3(0) = 0$$

Since the result is a true equality, the solution $x = -2$ is correct.

Inequalities are similar to equations, but instead of an equals sign, they have an inequality sign (either $>$, $<$, $\geq$, $\leq$, or $\neq$.) Linear inequalities are solved in the same way as linear equations. The only difference is that when multiplying or dividing by a negative number, the inequality sign must be flipped (i.e. $>$ becomes $<$, $\geq$ becomes $\leq$.)

For example, the inequality $-3t < 6$ can be solved by dividing both sides by -3, then flipping the inequality sign:

$$-3t < 6$$

$$\frac{-3t}{-3} > \frac{6}{-3}$$

$$t > -2$$

Recall that a linear equation is an equation in which none of the variables have exponents greater than 1. However, a linear equation can have multiple variables. If it does, the equation may not necessarily have one numerical solution. In fact, to solve an equation with more than one variable requires more than one equation.

Specifically, if given two variables, there must be two equations to solve; if three variables, then three equations are needed, etc.

A set of multiple linear equations with multiple variables is called a system of linear equations. Because a system of linear equations has multiple variables, its solution will be a list of values for each variable in the system. For instance, the solution to the system of equations shown below is $a = 1$ and $b = 3$; substituting both values into the equations below will result in two true equalities:

$$a + b = 4$$
$$a - b = -2$$

There are two methods for solving a system of linear equations: substitution and elimination. The substitution method is convenient to use when one of the equations is in the form *variable = expression* (or vice versa), and the isolated variable does not appear anywhere on the other side. For instance, in the linear system below, the first equation is in this form, so the substitution method can be used to solve it:

$$x = 4y - 1$$
$$2x - 3 = 3y$$

Solve this system by substituting $4y - 1$ for x into the second equation:

$$2(4y - 1) - 3 = 3y$$

Since the result is a linear equation with one variable, it can be solved for y using the process for solving a single variable linear equation. Once the value of y is found, substitute that value in either original equation and solve for the other variable, x.

Unfortunately, substitution is convenient for only a relatively limited number of situations. In many cases, a method called elimination (or combining equations) will be faster. To use the elimination method, add or subtract two equations in order to eliminate a variable. Linear systems like the example below are ideal candidates for the elimination method because the term $3n$ appears in the first equation and its opposite, $-3n$, is in the second equation:

$$4m + 3n = 5$$
$$m - 3n = 5$$

Adding the two equations together will cause the n-terms to cancel out:

$$\begin{array}{r} 4m + 3n = 5 \\ \underline{m - 3n = 5} \\ 5m + 0 = 10 \end{array}$$

As with the substitution method, the result is a linear equation with one variable, so it can be solved for m using the process discussed above. Substitute the value for m in either original equation and solve the result for n.

For a system of equations in which the coefficients of the variables are not opposites, the elimination method can still be used by multiplying one or more of the equations by a constant to get the coefficients into this form. In the example below, multiplying the first equation by 2 and the second equation by 3, will yield coefficients of the x-terms that will be opposites which can be added and cancelled:

$$\begin{aligned} 3x + 5y &= -1 \\ -2x + 6y &= 10 \end{aligned} \quad \rightarrow \quad \begin{aligned} 2(3x + 5y &= -1) \\ 3(-2 + 6y &= 10) \end{aligned} \quad \rightarrow \quad \begin{aligned} 6x + 10y &= -2 \\ -6x + 18y &= 30 \end{aligned}$$

Linear Equations, Inequalities and Systems Questions

1. If $2 - 4(x + 3) = 6$, then $x = ?$
   a. -4
   b. -1
   c. 1
   d. 4

2. If $3a = 2a + a + 4a - 4$, then $a = ?$
   a. 0
   b. 1
   c. $\frac{5}{2}$
   d. 3

3. Which of the following expressions is equivalent to $4 - \frac{1}{3}y > 5$?
   a. $y < -27$
   b. $y < -3$
   c. $y > -3$
   d. $y > 27$

4. If $x + 3y = 3$ and $-x + y = 5$, then $x = ?$
   a. -3
   b. -2
   c. 2
   d. 3

5. If $x = 2y - 3$ and $2x + \frac{1}{2}y = 3$, then $y = ?$
   a. $-\frac{2}{3}$
   b. 1
   c. 2
   d. $\frac{18}{7}$

Quadratic Expressions and Equations

This section measures the ability to correctly manipulate quadratic expressions and solve quadratic equations. Quadratic expressions are special types of expressions built out of monomials and polynomials.

A monomial is a single number, a variable, or the product of one or more numbers and variables with positive integer exponents. For example, the terms $\sqrt{3}$ and $\frac{4}{7}ab^5$ are both monomials, whereas the terms $\frac{4}{x^2}$ and $t^{\frac{3}{2}}$ are not since $\frac{4}{x^2}$ contains division by a variable, and $t^{\frac{3}{2}}$ has a non-integer exponent.

A series of multiple monomials separated by addition and subtraction signs form a type of expression called a polynomial. The expressions shown below are both examples of polynomials because all of their terms are valid monomials:

$$\frac{2}{3}xy^5z - \pi x^2 + 4 \qquad 2a^4 + 0.05a^3 - a^2 - 12.1a + 3$$

If a polynomial contains two monomials, it is called a binomial. If a polynomial contains three monomials, it is called a trinomial.

This section focused on how to manipulate quadratic expressions and equations. A quadratic expression is a polynomial of degree 2. In other words, it is a polynomial whose highest degree is 2. The degree of a monomial is defined as the sum of all the exponents on its variables. For example, the degree of $5xy^4z^2$ is 7 because $1 + 4 + 2 = 7$. Therefore, a quadratic expression is an expression in which every monomial either has degree 0, 1, or 2. Furthermore, a quadratic equation is an equation constructed only of quadratic expressions.

Any of the four main operations (addition, subtraction, multiplication, and division) can be performed on two or more polynomials. Two polynomials can be added or subtracted by setting up the operation vertically, aligning like terms, and then adding or subtracting like terms.

To multiply a constant by a polynomial, use the distributive property. Although the distributive property is usually given in the form $a(b + c) = ab + ac$, it can be extended to include polynomials with many monomials. For example, to distribute the expression $3(2a^3 + a^2 - 7)$, multiply the 3 by the coefficient of each term inside the parentheses and then simplify the result:

$$3(2a^3 + a^2 - 7) = (3 \cdot 2a^3) + (3 \cdot a^2) + [3 \cdot (-7)]$$
$$= 6a^3 + 3a^2 - 21$$

To multiply two binomials together, use the "FOIL" method. FOIL is an acronym that stands for "First, Outer, Inner, Last." This specifies the four products that must be calculated in order to complete the multiplication. First multiply the first terms of the binomial, then multiply the outer terms of the binomials, then multiply the inner terms of the binomials, and finally multiply the last terms of the binomials. Rules for multiplying terms with positive and/or negative signs must be carefully observed.

For instance, to multiply $(2x - 3)(x + 6)$, calculate the four FOIL products as follows:

The product of the First terms of $(\mathbf{2x} - 3)(\mathbf{x} + 6)$ is $2x \cdot x = 2x^2$.
The product of the Outer terms of $(\mathbf{2x} - 3)(x + \mathbf{6})$ is $2x \cdot 6 = 12x$.
The product of the Inner terms of $(2x - \mathbf{3})(\mathbf{x} + 6)$ is $(-3) \cdot x = -3x$.
The product of the Last terms of $(2x - \mathbf{3})(x + \mathbf{6})$ is $(-3) \cdot 6 = -18$.

Next, add the four products together and simplify the result by combining like terms:

$$(2x - 3)(x + 6) = 2x^2 + 12x - 3x - 18$$
$$= 2x^2 + 9x - 18$$

The opposite of multiplying polynomials is a process called factoring. In this section, some problems will require factoring a trinomial into a product of two binomials. Based on the example above, the factorization of $2x^2 + 9x - 18$ is the product $(2x - 3)(x + 6)$.

When factoring a polynomial, start by determining if the coefficients of the terms have a common factor. If so, find their greatest common factor (GCF) and factor it out. For example, the coefficients of the trinomial in the example below are 4, 16, and -84, which have a GCF of 4. Factor the 4 out by dividing the coefficient of each term by 4 (without changing the variables), and leaving the resulting values in parentheses:

$$4x^2 + 16x - 84 = 4(x^2 + 4x - 21)$$

Notice that the expression in parentheses is a trinomial in the form $ax^2 + bx + c$ with $a = 1$. Trinomials in this form are sometimes able to be factored. If a factorization does exist, it will be the product of two binomials in the form $(x + a)(x + b)$. To find the values of a and b, find two numbers whose sum is the coefficient of the x-term and whose product is the constant, c. In the example above, the coefficient of the x-term is 4 and the constant is -21. Therefore, a and b should be -3 and 7. Substitute these values into the format $(x + a)(x + b)$ to obtain the factorization of the trinomial. This factorization replaces the value in parentheses as shown:

$$4(x^2 + 4x - 21) = 4(x - 3)(x + 7)$$

Trinomials in the form $ax^2 + bx + c$ can sometimes be factored even if a > 1. In this case the factorization will be the product of two binomials in the form $(ax + b)(cx + d)$. The values of $a, b, c,$ and d can be found using trial-and-error. For a and c, consider all integer combinations whose product is the coefficient of the x^2-term. Similarly, for b and d, consider all integer combinations whose product is the constant, c. For instance, to factor the trinomial $9x^2 + 6x - 8$, the following combinations may be tried:

$$(3x + 8)(3x - 1) = 9x^2 + 21x - 8$$
$$(9x + 4)(x - 2) = 9x^2 - 14x - 8$$

Unfortunately, neither combination is correct since neither gives $6x$ as the middle term of the trinomial. Continuing with possible combinations will yield the following correct factorization of the trinomial:

$$9x^2 + 6x - 8 = (3x + 4)(3x - 2)$$

In addition, you can also factor binomials if they are the difference of two squares. A binomial is said to be the difference of two squares if it is in the form $a^2 - b^2$. For instance, $4c^2 - 81$ is the difference of two squares because the first term, $4c^2$, is the square of $2c$ and the second term, 81, is the square of 9. Factor binomials in this form using the rule $a^2 - b^2 = (a - b)(a + b)$:

$$4c^2 - 81 = (2c - 9)(2c + 9)$$

Lastly, this section will include questions that involve solving quadratic equations. Most of the time, quadratic equations will have two possible solutions. To solve a quadratic equation, move all the terms to one side and simplify the result. The result will be an equation in the form *quadratic expression = 0*. Next factor the expression on the left side using one of the methods described above.

Once the expression is factored, solve it by using the zero-product rule. The zero-product rule states that if the product of two expressions is zero, then one of the expressions must be zero. In other words, once the equation is factored, set each factor equal to zero and solve the resulting equation.

For example, to solve the equation $4c^2 - 81 = 0$, factor the quadratic expression on the left side, then set each factor equal to zero and solve those equations.

$$4c^2 - 81 = 0$$

$$(2c - 9)(2c + 9) = 0$$

$$2c - 9 = 0 \quad \text{or} \quad 2c + 9 = 0$$

$$c = \frac{9}{2} \qquad\qquad c = -\frac{9}{2}$$

Therefore, the possible solutions to the equation are $c = -\frac{9}{2}$ and $c = \frac{9}{2}$. Each solution must be verified by plugging the value into the original equation. In this case, both are valid solutions.

Quadratic Expressions and Equations Questions

1. $(y^2 + 9y - 2) + (4y^2 - y - 5) =$
   a. $5y^2 + 8y - 7$
   b. $5y^2 + 8y + 10$
   c. $5y^2 + 10y - 7$
   d. $5y^2 + 10y + 10$

2. $(x + 3)(x - 1) =$
   a. $x^2 - 3$
   b. $x^2 + 2$
   c. $x^2 - 3x + 2$
   d. $x^2 + 2x - 3$

3. $2c^2 - 32 =$
   a. $(c - 16)^2$
   b. $2(c + 4)^2$
   c. $(c - 16)(c + 16)$
   d. $2(c - 4)(c + 4)$

4. If $x^2 + 5x = 6$, then $x = ?$
   a. -6 or -1
   b. -6 or 1
   c. -1 or 6
   d. 1 or 6

5. If $2n^2 + 9n + 4 = 0$, then $n = ?$
   a. -4 or -2
   b. -4 or $-\frac{1}{2}$
   c. -2 or $-\frac{1}{4}$
   d. $-\frac{1}{4}$ or $-\frac{1}{2}$

Algebraic Expressions and Equations

This section measures the ability to correctly manipulate algebraic expressions and equations using the rules of algebra. A significant part of this requires an understanding of the basic concepts of algebra and its terminology. One of the most fundamental concepts in algebra is the concept of a variable.

A variable is a symbol that represents an unknown quantity. Variables are typically represented by English letters such as a, b, c, x, and y. In some contexts, Greek letters like α and θ are used. Conversely, a constant is a specific number or value such as 4.5, $-\frac{97}{203}$, or $2\sqrt{3}$. Some often-used numbers (e.g. π and e) are represented by letters even though they are constants, not variables.

The combination of variables and constants connected by one or more arithmetic operations form something called an algebraic expression. Expressions can appear in a wide variety of forms as the five examples below demonstrate:

$$5x \qquad 9a + \frac{7}{2}b - 4 \qquad 63.2m^4n \div \pi \qquad \frac{5}{z^{1/2}} \qquad 9\sqrt{t} - u$$

Expressions can be divided into smaller subunits called terms. For instance, the expression $9a + \frac{7}{2}b - 4$ is made up of three terms, $9a$, $\frac{7}{2}b$, and 4 that are separated by addition or subtraction signs. The number at the beginning of a term with a variable is called its coefficient. The coefficient of $9a$ is 9, and the coefficient of $\frac{7}{2}b$ is the fraction $\frac{7}{2}$. When the coefficient is not shown, it is equal to 1 since one times any number is the number itself.

An expression does not contain an equal sign (=) or an inequality sign (>, <, $\geq$, $\leq$, or $\neq$.) These signs indicate an equation or an inequality, not an expression; equations and inequalities can be solved for an unknown value whereas expressions alone cannot. An equation (or inequality) is really a pair of expressions separated by an equal sign (or inequality sign.) Each expression on either side of the equal sign can be referenced as the left side or the right side of the equation.

The questions in this section involve algebraic expressions that contain one or more variables. In addition to the rules of arithmetic for performing calculations with numbers, this section requires manipulation of variables, terms, expressions, and equations. In particular, this section will test ability to evaluate algebraic expressions and determine whether a solution satisfies an equation.

An algebraic expression can be evaluated if numerical values are provided for each of its variables. To evaluate an expression, substitute the corresponding value for each occurrence of the variable and then calculate the result.

For instance, if $x = 3$ and $y = 5$, then the expression $\frac{2x^2y}{8-2x}$ can be evaluated as follows:

$$\frac{2x^2y}{8-2x} = \frac{2(3)^2(5)}{8-2(3)}$$

$$= \frac{2 \cdot 9 \cdot 5}{8-6}$$

$$= \frac{90}{2}$$

$$= 45$$

Along the same lines, a solution is said to satisfy an equation if evaluating the equation for that value results in a true equality. For example, the solution $a = 1$ satisfies the equation $2a = 2$ because when 1 is substituted for a in the equation, the result is $2 \cdot 1 = 2$, which is true.

In addition, this section will also test application of the four main operations (addition, subtraction, multiplication, division, and exponentiation) on algebraic terms.

Algebraic terms can only be added or subtracted if they are *like terms*. *Like terms* are terms that contain the same variables with the same exponents on the variables. The coefficients of the terms may differ, however. For instance, x^6y and $0.2yx^6$ are like terms because they both contain the variables x^6 and y. Like terms can be combined by adding or subtracting their coefficients and keeping the variables and exponents the same:

$$x^6y - 0.2yx^6 = 1x^6y - 0.2x^6y$$
$$= 0.8x^6y$$

On the other hand, any two terms can be multiplied or divided, even if they are not like terms. To do this, multiply corresponding parts of the terms (i.e. the coefficients and like variables) separately as in $2a \cdot 3ab = (2 \cdot 3)(a \cdot a)b = 6a^2b$. Even a constant and a term with a variable can be multiplied or divided (since constants are terms, too) by multiplying or dividing the constant by the coefficient of the term. After multiplication or division of terms, use one or more of the exponent rules to simplify the result.

An exponent (also called a power) is an operation that represents a constant or variable multiplied by itself some number of times (the value of the exponent.) For instance, 2^5 (read "two to the fifth power") means you multiply 2 by itself five times. In this example, 2 is referred to as the base of exponent, and 5 is the exponent itself. Similarly, a^6 means you multiply a by itself six times. By default any variable without an exponent, has a power of 1 which means the value is just the variable itself.

Exponents can be applied to entire terms or expressions, not just single variables. In these situations, the exponent is distributed to each constant or variable within the expression (inside the parentheses.)

In the example below, this means that multiplying $6mn^2$ by itself four times is the same thing as distributing the exponent 4 among the three parts of the expression in parentheses, 6, m, and n^2:

$$(6mn^2)^4 = (6mn^2)(6mn^2)(6mn^2)(6mn^2)$$

$$= (6 \cdot 6 \cdot 6 \cdot 6)(m \cdot m \cdot m \cdot m)(n^2 \cdot n^2 \cdot n^2 \cdot n^2)$$

$$= 6^4 \cdot m^4 \cdot (n^2)^4$$

In addition to this, there are three main exponent rules that you should know for this section that will help you simplify expressions containing an exponent. First, to multiply exponential expressions with the same base, keep the base the same and add the exponents. For instance, since t^4 and t^2 have the same base, you can multiply them by adding their exponents:

$$t^4 \cdot t^2 = t^{4+2}$$
$$= t^6$$

Similarly, to divide exponential expressions with the same base, do the same thing, except subtract the exponents instead of adding them. Thus, to divide y^8 by y^3, subtract 3 from 8 and use the result as the new exponent of y:

$$y^8 \div y^3 = y^{8-3}$$
$$= y^5$$

Third, to raise an exponential expression to a power, multiply the two exponents together. For example, to raise a^3 to the fifth power, multiply 3 by 5:

$$(a^3)^5 = a^{3 \cdot 5}$$

- 34 -

$$= a^{15}$$

Finally, there is one more rule of algebra required to complete the problems in this section. To multiply a term by an expression that contains more than one term, distribute the first term over every term in the expression. In other words, multiply the first term by each term in the expression and then simplify the result. For instance, to simplify $-4a(5x - 2)$, distribute the $-4a$ by multiplying it by each term in parentheses (i.e. $5x$ and -2):

$$-4a(5x - 2) = (-4a \cdot 5x) + [-4a \cdot (-2)]$$
$$= -20ax + 8a$$

When distributing, it is crucial to keep track of the positive and negative signs of every term. Students often make the mistake of distributing the example above by either losing the negative sign on $-4a$ when multiplying it by -2 or losing the negative sign on -2:

$$-4a(5x - 2) \neq (-4a \cdot 5x) + [4a \cdot (-2)]$$
$$-4a(5x - 2) \neq (-4a \cdot 5x) + (-4a \cdot 2)$$

Either mistake will give the result $-20ax - 8a$, which is incorrect.

Algebraic Expressions and Equations Questions

1. What is the value of $2x^2 + 5x - y^2$ when $x = 3$ and $y = 5$?
   a. -4
   b. 8
   c. 16
   d. 72

2. Which of the following solutions satisfies the equation $5x = 15$?
   a. $x = 2$
   b. $x = 3$
   c. $x = 5$
   d. $x = 10$

3. If $a \neq 0$, then $12a^2b \div 3a = ?$
   a. $4b$
   b. $4ab$
   c. $9b^2$
   d. $9ab$

4. $(4x^5)^2 =$
   a. $4x^{10}$
   b. $4x^{25}$
   c. $8x^{25}$
   d. $16x^{10}$

5. $4x + 3(2y - x) =$
   a. $x + 6y$
   b. $3x + 6y$
   c. $4x + 3y$
   d. $7xy$

Word Problems and Applications

This section measures the ability to correctly use the algebraic skills tested so far in the form of word problems. This requires correctly interpreting information given in sentence format and using the skills tested in the rest of the section, including performing calculations with real numbers, manipulating and evaluating algebraic expressions, and solving linear and quadratic equations.

Word problems ask questions about real-life situations. The first step is to interpret the information given in the problem and formulate a plan to answer the question. In the most straightforward case, this plan may just involve performing a calculation with real numbers. But more likely, a multi-step process must be used, creating variables for an unknown numbers, setting up an equation containing that variable, solving the equation, and then interpreting the solution in the context of the original word problem. In some instances, a system of multiple equations each having multiple variables may be needed, which can be solved using either the elimination method or the substitution method.

After solving a word problem, it is a good idea to carefully reread the original problem to make sure that the solution took into account all necessary information, and is a valid solution. Be certain to provide the exact information requested in the word problem.

Word Problems and Applications Questions

1. The volume of a rectangular box is found by multiplying its length, width, and height. If the dimensions of a box are $\sqrt{3}$, $2\sqrt{5}$, and 4, what is its volume?
   a. $2\sqrt{60}$
   b. $4\sqrt{15}$
   c. $8\sqrt{15}$
   d. $24\sqrt{5}$

2. A cab ride costs $3.60 for the first half-mile and $0.75 for each additional mile. If d represents the distance travelled in miles, which expression represents the total cost of the cab ride in dollars ?
   a. $2.85 + 0.75d$
   b. $2.85 + 0.75(d - 0.5)$
   c. $3.60 + 0.75d$
   d. $3.60 + 0.75(d - 0.5)$

3. Adam has 24 coins worth $3.30. If the coins consist of dimes and quarters, how many dimes does Adam have?
   a. 6 dimes
   b. 10 dimes
   c. 16 dimes
   d. 18 dimes

4. The length of Square A is 3 feet longer than the length of Square B. If the difference between their areas is 75 ft², what is the length of Square B?
   a. 11 feet
   b. 12 feet
   c. 13 feet
   d. 14 feet

5. A metal ball is thrown up in the air from an initial height of 3 feet. Its height above the ground, in feet, t seconds after it is thrown is given by the expression $-16t^2 + 47t + 3$. How long will it take (in seconds) for the ball to hit the ground after it is thrown?
   a. $\frac{1}{16}$ seconds
   b. 1 second
   c. 3 seconds
   d. $4\frac{1}{2}$ seconds

College Level Mathematics

Algebraic Operations

This section measures the ability to simplify the result of various algebraic operations, including multiplication and division of polynomials, factoring, exponents, and radicals. Some of the problems in this section will involve concepts such as rational expressions and fractional exponents. In others, these more familiar concepts will be treated in more complicated ways.

Students should know the procedure for factoring trinomials in the form $ax^2 + bx + c$. Substitution can be used to extend this procedure to allow factoring polynomials such as $x^{10} + 6x^5 + 8$, in other words, polynomials whose degree is greater than 2. To use the substitution method, create a temporary variable (traditionally u, but any letter can be used) and set it equal to the variable in the trinomial to a power that is half of the degree of the trinomial. For example, to factor $x^{10} + 6x^5 + 8$, use $u = x^5$ (since 5 is half of 10) for the temporary variable.

Next, substitute u into the equation where possible. The result will be a trinomial whose only variable is u. It may make the substitution easier if the monomial is rewritten before substituting. For example, if $= x^5$, rewrite each monomial to show the x^5 explicitly and only after that would you substitute in u for x^5:

$$x^{10} + 6x^5 + 8 = (x^5)^2 + 6(x^5) + 8$$
$$= u^2 + 6u + 8$$

After substituting, the result will be a trinomial in the form $au^2 + bu + c$. Therefore, if it is factorable, the factorization will be the product of two binomials in the form $(au + b)(cu + d)$:

$$u^2 + 6u + 8 = (u + 2)(u + 4)$$

While this is a correct factorization of the trinomial, the ultimate factorization should not contain the temporary variable since u was only created to make the factorization easier. Eliminate the temporary variable using reverse of the substitution performed before. In this example, substitute x^5 for every occurrence of u in the factorization:

$$(u + 2)(u + 4) = (x^5 + 2)(x^5 + 4)$$

The result is one factorization of the original trinomial. Although it is not the case in this example, it may be possible to factor the result further, for instance if one of the factors is the difference of two squares.

A rational algebraic expression is the quotient of two polynomials. For instance, the expressions $\frac{5x}{8ax+b}$ and $\frac{x^2+5x+6}{3x+6}$ are both rational expressions. Rational expressions are very similar to fractions, except that they contain variables and exponents instead of just integers. A rational expression can be simplified using a method similar to the one used to simplify fractions. Specifically, a rational expression can be simplified by dividing the numerator and denominator by the same expression.

In this technique, that expression must be a factor of both the numerator and denominator. The first step is to factor the numerator and denominator as much as possible. Next, cancel out any common expressions that appear in both the numerator and denominator by dividing them both by the common expression.

For instance, to simplify the rational expression $\frac{x^2+5x+6}{3x+6}$, factor the numerator and denominator and then cancel out the common factor $(x+2)$:

$$\frac{x^2+5x+6}{3x+6} = \frac{(x+3)(x+2)}{3(x+2)}$$

$$= \frac{x+3}{3}$$

The FOIL method (a technique used to multiply two binomials) can be extended to allow you to expand more complicated expressions, such as $(a^2 - 5a)(3a - 2b + 4)$, which is the product of a binomial and a trinomial. To expand the product of two polynomials with any number of terms, multiply each term in the first polynomial by the second polynomial (in its entirety) as in the example below:

$$(a^2 - 5a)(3a - 2b + 4) = a^2(3a - 2b + 4) - 5a(3a - 2b + 4)$$

Next, distribute each product and combine like terms in the result:

$$a^2(3a - 2b + 4) - 5a(3a - 2b + 4)$$
$$= (3a^3 - 2a^2b + 4a^2) + (-15a^2 + 10ab - 20a)$$
$$= 3a^3 - 11a^2 - 20a + 10ab - 2a^2b$$

As with the FOIL method, it is important to keep track of the positive and negative signs throughout the whole process to arrive at the correct result.

Finally, to complete this section, students must be able to manipulate exponents and radicals with greater complexity than in elementary algebra. In particular, students should know how to work with negative exponents and understand the relationship between exponents and roots.

Recall that the reciprocal of an expression is a fraction with 1 in the numerator and the original expression in the denominator. For instance, the reciprocal of m is $\frac{1}{m}$. In addition to that notation, the reciprocal of any expression can be written using an exponent of -1. As an example, the expression m^{-1} is another way to write the reciprocal of m, so $m^{-1} = \frac{1}{m}$. Raising a number or expression to any negative exponent is the same thing as raising it to a positive exponent and then taking the reciprocal of the result: $a^{-4} = \frac{1}{a^4}$.

The word *root* (as in square root) has the same meaning as the word *radical*. The nth root of a number is the number that must be raised to the nth power to get the original number. For instance, the fifth root of 32, written as $\sqrt[5]{32}$, is equal to 2 because $2^5 = 32$. In this example, the 5 is called the degree of the root and 32 is called the radicand.

Any root can be converted to an expression with a rational exponent (and vice versa) by using the rule $a^{\frac{m}{n}} = \left(\sqrt[n]{a}\right)^m = \sqrt[n]{a^m}$. This rule says that when converting a rational exponent to a root, the degree of the root comes from the denominator of the exponent, and the new exponent comes from the numerator. This rule can be used to calculate the value of complicated expressions involving rational exponents like the example below:

$$4^{\frac{3}{2}} = \left(\sqrt[2]{4}\right)^3$$

$$= 2^3$$

$$= 8$$

Algebraic Operations Questions

1. $y^4 + 3y^2 - 4 =$
    a. $(y^3 - 4)(y + 1)$
    b. $(y^3 + 1)(y - 4)$
    c. $(y^2 + 1)(y - 2)(y + 2)$
    d. $(y^2 + 4)(y - 1)(y + 1)$

2. If $x \neq 5$, then $\frac{x^2 - 3x - 10}{4x - 20} = ?$

    a. $\frac{x - 5}{5}$

    b. $\frac{x - 2}{4}$

    c. $\frac{x + 2}{4}$

    d. $\frac{x^2 - 3x - 10}{4}$

3. $(2n^2 + 3n + 1)^2 =$
    a. $4n^4 + 6n^2 + 2$
    b. $4n^4 + 9n^2 + 1$
    c. $4n^4 + 6n^3 + 4n^2 + 3n + 1$
    d. $4n^4 + 12n^3 + 13n^2 + 6n + 1$

4. $(4a)^{-2} =$
    a. $\frac{1}{4a^2}$

    b. $\frac{1}{16a^2}$

    c. $2\sqrt{a}$

    d. $16\sqrt{a}$

5. $3^{\frac{5}{2}} - 3^{\frac{3}{2}} =$
    a. $3\sqrt{3}$
    b. $3\sqrt{5}$
    c. $6\sqrt{3}$
    d. $6\sqrt{5}$

Solutions of Equations and Inequalities

This section measures the ability to solve different types of equations and inequalities using algebraic methods. This section builds on techniques already developed in elementary algebra, but will focus on algebraic equations and inequalities that require more complicated methods to solve.

To solve a quadratic equation, first move everything to one side of the equation and then try to factor the result. There are three different methods used to factor a quadratic expression: factoring out a monomial, factoring a trinomial in the form $ax^2 + bx + c$ into the product of two binomials, or factoring the difference of two squares.

However, some quadratic equations cannot be factored with any of these methods. If a quadratic equation in the form $ax^2 + bx + c = 0$ cannot be factored, use the quadratic formula to solve it:

$$x = \frac{-b \pm \sqrt{b^2 - 4ac}}{2a}$$

The variables a, b, and c are the coefficients of the original trinomial.

For instance, to solve the equation $2x^2 - 2x - 7 = 0$, substitute $a = 2$, $b = -2$, and $c = -7$ into the quadratic formula and then simplify the result:

$$x = \frac{-(-2) \pm \sqrt{(-2)^2 - 4(2)(-7)}}{2(2)}$$

$$= \frac{2 \pm \sqrt{4 + 56}}{4}$$

$$= \frac{2 \pm \sqrt{60}}{4}$$

$$= \frac{2 \pm 2\sqrt{15}}{4}$$

$$= \frac{1}{2} \pm \frac{\sqrt{15}}{2}$$

Therefore, the solutions to the equation are $x = \frac{1}{2} - \frac{\sqrt{15}}{2}$ and $x = \frac{1}{2} + \frac{\sqrt{15}}{2}$.

Next, recall that an inequality is a mathematical statement that contains an inequality sign (either >, <, ≥, ≤, or ≠.) In most cases, the solution to a quadratic inequality will be a solution set defined by an inequality (or set of inequalities), such as $-4 < x < 9$ or $x \leq 1$ or $x \geq 7$. To find the solution set of a quadratic equation, the first step is to change the inequality sign to an equal sign (=) and solve the resulting equation by either factoring or using the quadratic formula.

For instance, solve the inequality $x^2 + x - 2 \leq 0$ by re-writing the inequality as an equation and solving that for x:

$$x^2 + x - 2 = 0$$

$$(x + 2)(x - 1) = 0$$

$$x + 2 = 0 \quad \text{or} \quad x - 1 = 0$$

$$x = -2 \qquad\qquad x = 1$$

Most quadratic equations have two solutions. These two solutions divide the number line into three regions. In the example above, the two solutions, $x = -2$ and $x = 1$, divide the number line into the three regions: $x < -2$, $-2 < x < 1$, and $x > 1$. To determine which regions are part of the solution set, pick a test value from each and substitute it in the original inequality. If the result is a true inequality, then the whole region is part of the solution set. Otherwise, the whole region is not part in the solution set. For the example, choose the numbers $x = -3$, $x = 0$, and $x = 2$ as the three test values and then test them:

Region	Test Value	$x^2 + x - 2 \leq 0$	Conclusion
$x < -2$	-3	$(-3)^2 + (-3) - 2 \leq 0$ $9 - 3 - 2 \leq 0$ $4 \leq 0$	Not part of the solution set
$-2 < x < 1$	0	$(0)^2 + (0) - 2 \leq 0$ $-2 \leq 0$	Part of the solution set
$x > 1$	2	$(2)^2 + (2) - 2 \leq 0$ $4 + 2 - 2 \leq 0$ $4 \leq 0$	Not part of the solution set

Based upon these results, only one of the regions, $-2 < x < 1$, is part of the solution set. Furthermore, since the original inequality sign was a less-than-or-equal-to sign (rather than just a less-than sign), the solution set contains the points x = −2 and x = 1 as well. Therefore, the solution set is $-2 \leq x \leq 1$.

A system of equations is a set of multiple linear equations with multiple variables. This section requires solving systems with more than two equations and more than two variables. To solve systems like this, start by organizing the equations by writing them vertically with corresponding variables lined up. Next, label the equations with numbers for reference (e.g. Label the first equation as "equation (1)".) For example, given the system of three equations below, organize them as follows:

$$
\begin{array}{ll}
(1) & a + 2b - c = 7 \\
(2) & 3a \quad\quad + c = 1 \\
(3) & -4a - b \quad\quad = -6
\end{array}
$$

To solve a system of equations, use the elimination method. Although any number of equations can be added together at a time, it is usually more practical to only add two at a time. Next, add or subtract two equations so that the result is an equation that only contains the variables that appear in a third equation. For the example, add equations (1) and (2) in order to eliminate c, a variable which does not appear in equation (3):

$$
\begin{array}{ll}
(1) & a + 2b - c = 7 \\
(2) & \underline{3a \quad\quad + c = 1} \\
(4) & 4a + 2b \quad\quad = 8
\end{array}
$$

Next add equations (3) and (4) to eliminate the variable a:

$$
\begin{array}{ll}
(3) & -4a - b \quad = -6 \\
(4) & \underline{4a + 2b = 8} \\
& \quad\quad b \quad = 2
\end{array}
$$

Therefore, the solution for b is 2. Find the value of the other two variables by first substituting the value of b into equation (3) and solve the result for a. Then substitute the value of a into equation (2) and solve for c. The final solution is $a = 1$, $b = 2$, and $c = -2$. This general process can be used to solve systems of any number of equations and variables, but it becomes unwieldy very quickly as the number of equations and variables grow.

In addition, there are two other types of equations that are tested in this section: rational equations and radical equations. A rational equation is an equation in which some of the terms are fractions with a variable in their denominators. For instance, $x - \dfrac{6}{x-2} = 1$ is a rational equation because one term has $x - 2$ as its denominator. To solve a rational equation, eliminate the denominators by multiplying both sides of the equation by the denominator to cancel this value out.

For example, to solve $x - \frac{6}{x-2} = 1$, multiply both sides of by $(x - 2)$ and then simplify the result:

$$x - \frac{6}{x-2} = 1$$

$$(x - 2)\left[x - \frac{6}{x-2}\right] = (x - 2) \cdot 1$$

$$x(x - 2) - 6 = x - 2$$

$$x^2 - 2x - 6 = x - 2$$

Next solve the resulting equation for x:

$$x^2 - 3x - 4 = 0$$

$$(x + 1)(x - 4) = 0$$

$$x + 1 = 0 \quad \text{or} \quad x - 4 = 0$$

$$x = -1 \qquad\qquad x = 4$$

One thing that distinguishes rational equations from other types of equations is that some values of the variable result in division by zero. Therefore, when solving a rational equation, solutions must be checked to make sure that substituting them into the original equation does not cause division by zero. If so, they are not really solutions to the equation. In the example above, the original equation had $x - 2$ as one of its denominators. This expression is equal to zero only when $x = 2$, so the two solutions found, $x = -1$ and $x = 4$, do not cause division by zero and are valid solutions.

A radical equation has terms that are radicals and contain a variable. The equation $\sqrt{5x - 1} - 3 = 4$ is a radical equation because the radical $\sqrt{5x - 1}$ contains the variable x. Solve a radical equation by isolating the radical term and then squaring both sides of the equation to eliminate the radical. For example, to solve $\sqrt{5x - 1} - 3 = 4$, add 3 to both sides to isolate the radical term and then square both sides as follows:

$$\sqrt{5x - 1} - 3 = 4$$
$$\sqrt{5x - 1} = 7$$
$$(\sqrt{5x - 1})^2 = 49$$
$$5x - 1 = 49$$

Once the radical is removed, the equation can be solved for x:

$$5x = 50$$
$$x = 10$$

Note that when squaring both sides of an equation to find a solution for x, there is a risk of finding an incorrect solution. Substitute each solution into the original equation to determine if the solution is valid (produces a true equation.) For the example above, substitute the solution, $x = 10$, into the original equation:

$$\sqrt{5x - 1} - 3 = 4$$
$$\sqrt{5(10) - 1} - 3 = 4$$
$$\sqrt{49} - 3 = 4$$
$$7 - 3 = 4 \;\; True$$

Since the result of the substitution is a true equality, the solution $x = 10$ is correct.

Solutions of Equations and Inequalities Questions

1. If $4x^2 + 2x = 1$, then $x = ?$
   a. $-\frac{1}{8} \pm \frac{\sqrt{3}}{4}$
   b. $-\frac{1}{8} \pm \frac{\sqrt{5}}{4}$
   c. $-\frac{1}{4} \pm \frac{\sqrt{3}}{4}$
   d. $-\frac{1}{4} \pm \frac{\sqrt{5}}{4}$

2. Given $x^2 - 7x + 10 \geq 0$, what is the solution set for x?
   a. $2 \leq x \leq 5$
   b. $x \leq 2$ or $x \geq 5$
   c. $7 \leq x \leq 10$
   d. $x \leq 7$ or $x \geq 10$

3. If $x + 2y = 1, 3y + z = 1,$ and $-x + y + 3z = 8$, then $x = ?$
   a. 3
   b. 4
   c. 5
   d. 6

4. If $\frac{4}{x-3} - \frac{2}{x} = 1$, then $x = ?$
   a. -6
   b. -1
   c. -6 or -1
   d. -1 or 6

5. If $\sqrt{3x - 2} = x - 2$, then $x = ?$
   a. 1
   b. 6
   c. -1 or 6
   d. 1 or 6

Coordinate Geometry

This section measures the ability to solve problems involving coordinate geometry, or geometry involving the coordinate (or Cartesian) plane.

The coordinate plane relates geometric objects, like points and lines, to symbolic representations, like ordered pairs and equations. It is formed by the intersection of a horizontal number line (the x-axis) and a vertical number line (the y-axis) that meet at a point called the origin. These two axes divide the coordinate plane into four distinct regions called quadrants, which are labeled I, II, III, and IV as follows:

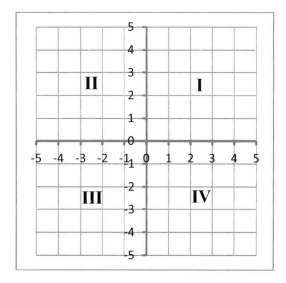

Based on the x- and y-axes, you can assign a unique pair of coordinates to every point in the plane. These coordinates are written as an ordered pair (x,y). The first number in the ordered pair, called the x-coordinate of the point, represents the point's distance to the left or right of the y-axis. If the x-coordinate is negative, then the point is to the left of the y-axis; if it is positive, then the point is to the right; if the value is zero then the point sits on the y-axis. The second number, called the y-coordinate of the point, represents the point's distance above or below the x-axis. If the y-coordinate is negative, then the point is below the x-axis; if it is positive, then the point is above the x-axis; if it is zero, then the point sits on the x-axis.

For instance, to graph (−2,4) on the coordinate grid, start at the origin and move 2 units to the left and then 4 units up. A dot on the grid at (-2,4) is used to represent this coordinate location graphically.

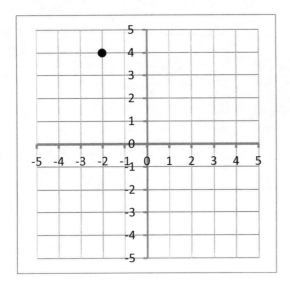

In addition to specific points, any equation can be graphed on the coordinate plane as long as it contains only the variables x and y. The graph of an equation is the set of points that satisfies the equation. If the graph of an equation is a line, then every point on that line represents a pair of values, x and y, that satisfies the original equation.

An equation can be graphed by substituting three or more values of x into the equation and then calculate the corresponding values of y. For convenience, these values can be organized into a table. For instance, to graph the equation $y = 2x - 3$, create a table of values like the one below:

x	$y = 2x - 3$	(x,y)
−1	$2(-1) - 3 = -5$	$(-1,-5)$
0	$2(0) - 3 = -3$	$(0,-3)$
1	$2(1) - 3 = -1$	$(1,-1)$

From the table, you can tell that the graph of this equation will pass through the points (−1,−5), (0,−3), and (1,−1). Graph the equation by plotting these three points table and then connecting them with a straight line that extends infinitely in either direction:

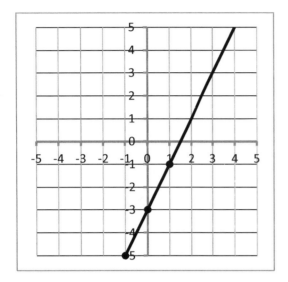

The graph of any linear equation is a straight line like the one above. Linear equations are often written in the form $y = mx + b$, which is called slope-intercept form because it can be used to easily determine the slope and y-intercept of the corresponding line. An equation in slope-intercept form $y = mx + b$ has a slope represented by the value m and a y-intercept represented by the value b.

The slope of a line is a measure of its steepness. A line that is nearly vertical has a very large slope (or a very small slope if it is negative), while a line that is horizontal or nearly horizontal has a slope that is closer to zero. If the line goes up as you go from left to right, then its slope is positive; if it goes down, the slope is negative. The slope can be calculated by choosing two points on the line, (x_1, y_1) and (x_2, y_2), and substituting the values of x_1, y_1, x_2, and y_2 into the equation $m = \frac{y_2 - y_1}{x_2 - x_1}$. In other words, compute the differences between the x- and y-coordinates and then divide the change in y by the change in x. For example, in the table of values above, the line $y = 2x - 3$ contains the points (0,−3) and (1,−1). Therefore, the slope of the line is $\frac{-1-(-3)}{1-0} = 2$, which confirms what the slope-intercept form of the equation also indicates, $m = 2$.

The relationship between the slopes of two lines can provide useful information about those lines. Two lines that have the same slope are parallel, that is they do not intersect no matter how far extended in either direction. The converse is also true: if two lines are parallel, then they must have the same slope. Two lines are perpendicular if and only if their slopes are negative reciprocals. For instance, if a given line has a slope of 3, then every line parallel to it also has a slope of 3 and every line perpendicular to it has a slope of $-\frac{1}{3}$.

The y-intercept of a line is the y-coordinate of the point where the line intercepts the y-axis. For instance, the graph of $y = 2x - 3$ intercepts the y-axis at the point $(0,-3)$. Therefore, its y-intercept is -3, which confirms what the slope-intercept form of the equation also indicates, $b = -3$. Although it doesn't come up very much, lines also have an x-intercept, which is defined as the x-coordinate of the point where the line intercepts the x-axis.

When an equation for a line is in slope-intercept form $y = mx + b$, the slope and y-intercept, which are given by the values of m and b, can be easily determined. Conversely, if given a slope and y-intercept of a line, the equation for that line can be determined by substituting these values back into the equation of the form $y = mx + b$.

While linear equations are always graphed as straight lines, the graph of a quadratic equation can be any one of the four conic sections. A conic section is a curve obtained by the intersection of a cone and a plane. In particular, the four conic sections are the circle, the ellipse, the parabola, and the hyperbola. The chart below gives a general equation for each of the four conic sections as well as an example of each.

Conic Section	Equation	Example
Circle	$(x - h)^2 + (y - k)^2 = r^2$	
Ellipse	$\dfrac{(x-h)^2}{a^2} + \dfrac{(y-k)^2}{b^2} = 1$	

Parabola	$(x - h)^2 = 4a(y - k)$	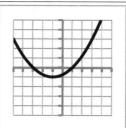
Hyperbola	$\dfrac{(x-h)^2}{a^2} - \dfrac{(y-k)^2}{b^2} = 1$	

Students must be able to graph inequalities on a coordinate plane as well. The graph of an inequality will not be a point, line, or curve; it will be a region represented by a shaded area. Every point in this region represents a pair of values, x and y, that satisfy the original inequality.

To graph an inequality, first graph its boundary line or lines: change the inequality sign to an equal sign and graph the result. If the original inequality contains a < or >, graph it with a dotted (or dashed) line to indicate that the points on the line are not part of the solution set; if the original inequality contains a ≤ or ≥, graph it with a solid line to indicate that the points are part of the solution set. For example, to graph $y > x + 1$, first graph the equation $y = x + 1$ with a dashed line:

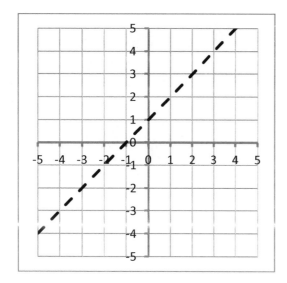

Next, shade the regions that are part of the solution set of the inequality. In the example above, shade either the region to the left of the dashed line or the region to the right of it. To choose which region to shade, choose test points in each of the regions. Then test these points by substituting their coordinates into the original inequality and simplifying the result. If the result is a true inequality, then the whole region that contains that test value should be shaded.

For the example above, test the point (0,0) (i.e. the origin) by substituting $x = 0$ and $y = 0$ into the original inequality:

$y \geq x + 1$
$(0) \geq (0) + 1$
$0 \geq 1$ *false*

Since the result is false, shade the other region of the graph, the region to the left of the line:

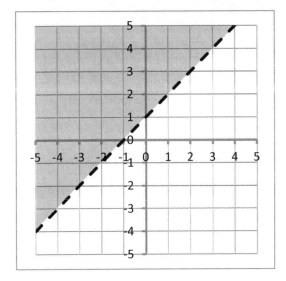

The resulting graph (including the shaded region, but not the dashed line), represents the solution set of the original inequality.

Coordinate Geometry Questions

1. What are the coordinates of vertices of the triangle below?

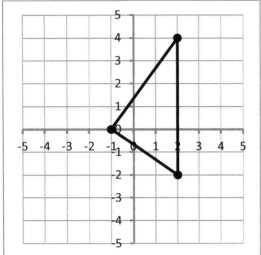

    a. $(-1,0)$, $(2,4)$, and $(2,-2)$
    b. $(-1,0)$, $(4,2)$, and $(2,-2)$
    c. $(0,-1)$, $(4,2)$, and $(-2,2)$
    d. $(0,-1)$, $(2,4)$, and $(-2,2)$

2. The equation of line L is $y = 3x + 4$. Which of the following is the equation of the line perpendicular to L that intersects at the point $(-3,-5)$?
    a. $y = -\frac{1}{3}x - 6$
    b. $y = -\frac{1}{3}x - 4$
    c. $y = \frac{1}{3}x - 6$
    d. $y = \frac{1}{3}x - 4$

3. What type of conic section does the equation $x^2 + y^2 = 11$ represent?
    a. Circle
    b. Ellipse
    c. Parabola
    d. Hyperbola

4. Which of the following graphs represents $y = x^2 + 2x - 1$?

a.

b.

c.

d.

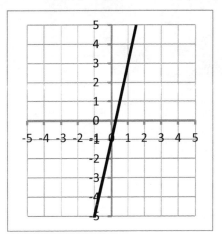

5. Which of the following graphs represents $y \leq 3x + 1$?

a.

b.

c.

d.

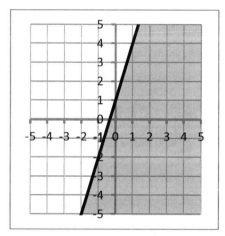

Applications and Other Algebra Topics

This section measures the ability to correctly solve problems involving advanced algebraic concepts such as complex numbers, sequences, permutations, and combinations. Some of the problems are word problems, therefore students must be able to interpret real-life situations while also applying these algebraic concepts correctly.

Based upon an understanding of the topics presented and the coordinate plane, equations like $x^2 + 1 = 0$ cannot be solved because any real number squared will always produce a positive number. However, in the 18th century, mathematicians started using a new number, represented by the letter i and defined as $\sqrt{-1}$, to solve equations such as this. Since $i = \sqrt{-1}$, it is also true that $i^2 = -1$. Therefore, the solutions of the equation $x^2 + 1 = 0$ are $x = i$ and $x = -i$.

Using the definition of i, the square root of any negative number can be rewritten as a real number times i. Numbers like this are called imaginary numbers. Some examples of imaginary numbers are $5i$, $\frac{3i}{2}$, and $2i\sqrt{5}$. Imaginary numbers are now universally accepted by mathematicians and have even found practical application in electrical engineering.

To simplify the square root of a negative number, rewrite it as the product of two radicals, $\sqrt{-1}$ and the square root of a positive number, and then simplify the result.

For example, $\sqrt{-27}$ can be simplified as follows:

$$\sqrt{-27} = \sqrt{-1} \times \sqrt{27}$$
$$= i \times 3\sqrt{3}$$
$$= 3i\sqrt{3}$$

The set of numbers that includes every real and imaginary number is the set of complex numbers. A complex number is any number that can be written in the form $a + bi$, where a and b are real numbers and i is the imaginary unit described above.

Complex numbers sometimes come up as solutions to quadratic equations. The quadratic formula (shown below), used to solve a quadratic equation in the form $ax^2 + bx + c = 0$, can demonstrate this:

$$x = \frac{-b \pm \sqrt{b^2 - 4ac}}{2a}$$

The quadratic formula contains a square root whose radicand is $b^2 - 4ac$. If this quantity (which is called the discriminant of the equation) is negative, the solution to the equation will be two complex numbers. In a more general sense, the discriminant of an equation can be used to determine the number and nature of the equation's solutions as follows:

1) If the discriminant is zero, then the equation has one real, rational solution.
2) If it is a positive perfect square, then the equation has two real, rational solutions.
3) If it is positive and not a perfect square, then the equation has two real, irrational solutions.
4) If it is negative, then the equation has two solutions that are complex conjugates (i.e. two complex numbers in the forms $a + bi$ and $a - bi$).

A sequence is a list of numbers. The numbers that make up the sequence are called its terms. For convenience, the notation a_1 is used for the first term of the sequence, the notation a_2 is used for the second term, and a_n represents the nth term of the sequence for any positive value of n. The terms of a sequence may be based on a pattern (i.e. a rule to get from one term to the next), or they may have no relationship to the other terms. In this section, two types of sequences that are infinitely long and based on simple rules will be covered.

An arithmetic sequence is a sequence in which each term is a specific constant more than the one before it. For instance, in the sequence below, each term can be found by adding -7 to the term before it:

$$16, 9, 2, -5, -12, -19, \ldots$$

The constant that must be added to each term to get the next one is called the common difference of the sequence and is represented by the variable d. In the example above, the common difference of the sequence is $d = -7$.

The nth term of an arithmetic sequence can be found by writing out each term of the sequence until reaching the nth term, however this can be very time consuming. A much easier way is to use the formula for the nth term of an arithmetic sequence:

$$a_n = a_1 + (n - 1)d$$

For example, to calculate the 40th term of the sequence above, substitute the values $n = 40$, $a_1 = 16$, and $d = -7$ into this formula and simplify the result:

$$\begin{aligned}
a_{40} &= 16 + (40 - 1) \cdot (-7) \\
&= 16 + 39 \cdot (-7) \\
&= -257
\end{aligned}$$

There is a method to calculate the sum of the first n terms of an arithmetic sequence, which is written as S_n. First calculate the sum of the first nine terms of the sequence above by writing out the terms explicitly:

$$S_9 = 16 + 9 + 2 + (-5) + (-12) + (-19) + (-26) + (-33) + (-40)$$

Note that specific pairs of terms add up to the same number: the first and last terms of the sequence add up to -24, the second and second-to-last terms add up to -24, and so on as shown below:

The sum of a_1 and a_9 is $16 + (-40) = -24$.
The sum of a_2 and a_8 is $9 + (-33) = -24$.
The sum of a_3 and a_7 is $2 + (-26) = -24$.
The sum of a_4 and a_6 is $(-5) + (-19) = -24$.

The one term not paired is $a_6 = -12$, which is exactly half of -24. Thus, the sum of the first nine terms of the sequence is $4\frac{1}{2}$ (or $\frac{9}{2}$) times the sum of a_1 and a_9:

$$\begin{aligned} S_9 &= \frac{9}{2}[16 + (-40)] \\ &= \frac{9}{2}(-24) \\ &= -108 \end{aligned}$$

The sum of the first n terms of an arithmetic sequence as demonstrated above can be generalized to provide a formula for S_n:

$$S_n = \frac{n}{2}(a_1 + a_n)$$

A second type of sequence that is tested in this section is called a geometric sequence. A geometric sequence is a sequence in which each term is a specific constant times the term before it. For example, in the sequence below, each term can be found by multiplying the preceding term by 3:

$$\frac{2}{9}, \frac{2}{3}, 2, 6, 18, 54, \dots$$

The constant that is multiplied with each term in a geometric sequence is called the common ratio of the sequence and is represented by the variable r. In the example above, the common ratio of the sequence is $r = 3$.

In addition, there are two formulas used to find specific values related to a given geometric sequence. The nth term of a geometric sequence can be found using the formula for a_n:

$$a_n = a_1 r^{n-1}$$

The sum of the first n terms of a geometric sequence can be found using the formula for S_n:

$$S_n = \frac{a_1(1-r^n)}{1-r}$$

The last topic in this section involves interpreting and solving word problems using permutations and combinations. A permutation is an arrangement of a set of objects in which the order of the objects does matter. For example, the first three letters of the alphabet can be combined into six distinct two-letter permutations as follows:

$$AB \quad AC \quad BA \quad BC \quad CA \quad CB$$

The notation $_nP_k$ gives the number of different permutations possible with a total of n objects to form a group of k objects without using an object more than once. The value of $_nP_k$ can be found using the formula below:

$$_nP_k = \frac{n!}{(n-k)!}$$

The exclamation mark (!) is the symbol for the factorial of a number. The factorial of a number is defined as the product of all the whole numbers less than or equal to it. The value of 7! is:

$$7! = 7 \times 6 \times 5 \times 4 \times 3 \times 2 \times 1$$
$$= 5040$$

On the other hand, a combination is an arrangement of a set of objects in which the order of the objects does not matter. For example, the first four letters of the alphabet can be arranged into four distinct three-letter combinations if letters are not used more than once. Since order does not matter, ABC and BAC are counted as the same combination:

$$ABC \quad ABD \quad ACD \quad BCD$$

The notation $\binom{n}{k}$ gives the number of different combinations possible among a total of n objects to form a group of k objects without using an object more than once. The value of $\binom{n}{k}$ can be found using the formula below:

$$\binom{n}{k} = \frac{n!}{k!(n-k)!}$$

Applications and Other Algebra Topics Questions

1. If $2x(x + 1) = -3$, then $x = ?$

 a. $-\frac{1}{2} \pm \frac{\sqrt{5}}{2}$

 b. $-\frac{1}{2} \pm \frac{\sqrt{7}}{2}$

 c. $-\frac{1}{2} \pm \frac{i\sqrt{5}}{2}$

 d. $-\frac{1}{2} \pm \frac{i\sqrt{7}}{2}$

2. What is the sum of the first 20 terms of the sequence 2, 5, 8, 11, ...?
 a. 59
 b. 61
 c. 590
 d. 610

3. There are 500 bacteria in a Petri dish. If the number of bacteria doubles every day, how many bacteria will be in the Petri dish in 14 days?
 a. 102,400
 b. 204,800
 c. 306,800
 d. 409,600

4. A committee of 12 people is electing four of its members for president, vice president, secretary, and treasurer. In how many different ways can they elect these four positions?
 a. 1680
 b. 9240
 c. 11,880
 d. 20,736

5. Using a standard deck, how many different five-card hands consist only of spades?
 a. 1287
 b. 6435
 c. 51,480
 d. 154,440

Functions and Trigonometry

This section measures the ability to correctly solve problems involving various types of functions and their properties. Functions are mathematical objects that return an output value for every valid input put into them. Functions assign exactly one output value to each input.

Functions are written in a notation called function notation. In function notation, $f(x)$ (read "f of x") represents a function called f whose input value is x. As an example, if the function f is defined as $(x) = x^2 + 5x$, then its output is the value of the expression $x^2 + 5x$ for any particular x-value in its domain. To calculate $f(x)$ for a specific value of x, substitute that value into $x^2 + 5x$ and then simplify the result:

$$
\begin{aligned}
f(-3) &= (-3)^2 + 5(-3) \\
&= 9 - 15 \\
&= -6
\end{aligned}
$$

The set of all possible input values that can be evaluated by a function is called the function's domain. Many functions can take any real numbers as an input value, so their domain is the set of all real numbers. Some examples of functions like this are shown below:

$$f(x) = 6x^2 + 3x - 4 \qquad g(x) = 3^x \qquad h(x) = \sqrt[3]{2x - 7} + 1$$

Other functions are only defined for a specific subset of all real numbers. One way to find the domain of a function is to look at all the different operations that are used in the function and determine if one or more of them is undefined for some values of the input. Then the domain of the function will be the set of all real numbers except those input values. For example, division by zero is undefined. Therefore, the domain of the function $f(x) = \frac{2}{x-1}$ is all real numbers except $x = 1$ which would cause division by zero. This particular domain is also sometimes written as $x \neq 1$.

Another way to find the domain of a function is to graph it on a coordinate plane. The domain of $f(x) = \sqrt{x}$ can be found by graphing the equation $= \sqrt{x}$. The domain of the f is the set of all x-values that the graph is defined for.

The set of all possible output values of the function is called the function's range. The range of a function can be found by graphing it on a coordinate plane. In the graph, the range of the function is the set of all y-values that the graph is defined for.

The inverse of a function is a function that undoes the original function. The inverse of $f(x) = 2x$ is $g(x) = \frac{x}{2}$ because, for any value of x, if $f(x) = y$, then $g(y) = x$. The inverse of $f(x)$ is notated as $f^{-1}(x)$, such as $f^{-1}(x) = \frac{x}{2}$. Many inverse functions can be determined intuitively; the inverse of "multiplying a number by 2" is "dividing a number by 2", therefore the inverse of $f(x) = 2x$ is $f^{-1}(x) = \frac{x}{2}$.

The inverse of a more complex functions, like $h(x) = \frac{3}{2x} + 7$, may not be as intuitive to find. In this case, start with the definition of $h(x)$ and then replace $h(x)$ with y:

$$h(x) = \frac{3}{2x} + 7$$
$$y = \frac{3}{2x} + 7$$

Next switch all the x's and y's and solve for y:

$$x = \frac{3}{2y} + 7$$
$$x - 7 = \frac{3}{2y}$$
$$2y(x - 7) = 3$$
$$2y = \frac{3}{x-7}$$
$$y = \frac{3}{2(x-7)}$$

Finally, replace y with $h^{-1}(x)$ to notate the inverse of the original function:

$$h^{-1}(x) = \frac{3}{2(x-7)}$$

The composition of two functions is a function formed by combining the two functions so that the output of one is the input of the other. The notation for the composition of two functions, $f(x)$ and $g(x)$, is $(f \circ g)(x)$, which is defined by the equation $(f \circ g)(x) = (f(g(x))$. To find the composition of two functions, substitute the output of the second function for the input of the first function and then simplify the result. For instance, if the functions f and g are defined as $f(x) = 3x + 1$ and $g(x) = 2x^2$, then the composition is:

$$(f \circ g)(x) = f(2x^2)$$
$$= 3(2x^2) + 1$$
$$= 6x^2 + 1$$

The problems in this section contain five different types of functions: polynomial, rational, exponential, logarithmic, and trigonometric functions. Students must be able to evaluate each of these types of functions for specific input values, identify the domain and range, find the inverse, and calculate the composition of two functions.

A polynomial function is a function that contains a polynomial. The function $f(x) = x^4 - \frac{1}{2}x + 3$ is an example of a polynomial function. The terms of a polynomial

- 65 -

function are usually written in descending order of exponents. Thus, the expression below is the general form for a polynomial function, in which the a's are constants and n is the largest exponent in the polynomial (i.e. the degree of the polynomial):

$$f(x) = a_n x^n + a_{n-1} x^{n-1} + \cdots + a_2 x^2 + a_1 x + a_0$$

An exponential function is a function in which the input variable is an exponent of a constant. The general form for an exponential function is $f(x) = a^x$, where a is a constant. An exponential function is not the same as a function in the form $f(x) = x^a$. Besides having different output values, the two also have different types of inverses. Whereas the inverse of a function like $f(x) = x^3$ is a radical function (a function containing a root of the input), in this case the cube root of x, the inverse of an exponential function is a logarithmic function (a function containing the logarithm of the input.)

The logarithm of a number x is the exponent that another number b must be raised to in order to get that number. The number b is called the base of the logarithm. Logarithms are notated as $\log_b x$ (read "the logarithm of x to base b"). For example, since $10^3 = 1000$, the value of $\log_{10} 1000$ is 3.

Trigonometric functions are functions of an angle that are based on the proportions of a right triangle. The input value for the functions, an angle, is usually represented by the Greek letter θ ("theta.") The three main trigonometric functions are sine, cosine, and tangent. They are defined as the ratios of the sides of a right triangle:

$$sin\ \theta\ = \frac{\text{opposite}}{\text{hypotenuse}} \qquad cos\ \theta\ = \frac{\text{adjacent}}{\text{hypotenuse}} \qquad tan\ \theta\ = \frac{\text{opposite}}{\text{adjacent}}$$

For example, in the right triangle below, the side opposite θ is 3 units long, the side adjacent to θ is 4 units long, and the hypotenuse of the triangle (the longest side) is 5 units long. Therefore, the values of trigonometric functions for the angle θ are $\theta = \frac{3}{5}$, $cos\ \theta = \frac{4}{5}$, and $tan\ \theta = \frac{3}{4}$.

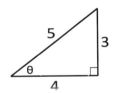

The mnemonic SOH-CAH-TOA can be used to help remember the definitions of the three trigonometric functions. SOH-CAH-TOA stands for "Sine = Opposite ÷ Hypotenuse, Cosine = Adjacent ÷ Hypotenuse, Tangent = Opposite ÷ Adjacent."

Functions and Trigonometry Questions

1. If $f(x) = 4x^3 + 5x^2 - 2$, then $f\left(-\frac{1}{2}\right) = ?$

   a. $-\frac{13}{2}$

   b. $-\frac{15}{4}$

   c. $-\frac{5}{4}$

   d. $-\frac{1}{4}$

2. What is the domain of $(x) = \frac{4}{x+2}$?

   a. $x \neq -2$
   b. $x < 4$
   c. $x \geq 2$
   d. All Real Numbers

3. If $f(x) = 2x - 4$ and $g(x) = \frac{3x+1}{2}$, then $(f \circ g)(x) = ?$

   a. $3x - \frac{11}{2}$

   b. $3x - 3$

   c. $6x - \frac{11}{2}$

   d. $6x - 3$

4. If $h(x) = \log_{10}(x + 2)$, then $h^{-1}(x) = ?$
   a. 10^{x-2}
   b. 10^{x+2}
   c. $10^x - 2$
   d. $10^x + 2$

5. If θ is an acute angle and $\sin\theta = \frac{5}{7}$, then $\cos\theta = ?$

   a. $\frac{2}{7}$

   b. $\frac{2}{5}$

   c. $\frac{4}{7}$

   d. $\frac{2\sqrt{6}}{7}$

Answer Key

Arithmetic

Computations with Integers and Fractions

1. A: According to the order of operations (PEMDAS), first subtract to find the value in the parentheses, then multiply the result by 5, and finally divide by 3:

$$5(3-9) \div 3 = 5(-6) \div 3$$

$$= -30 \div 3$$

$$= -10$$

2. B: According to the order of operations (PEMDAS), first simplify the numerator and the denominator of the expression, then perform the division:

$$\frac{4-(-12)}{-9+5} = \frac{4+12}{-9+5}$$

$$= \frac{16}{-4}$$

$$= -4$$

3. A: According to the order of operations (PEMDAS), start with the expression in parentheses. To add two fractions, rewrite them with a common denominator and then add the numerators. Keep in mind that the first fraction is negative and the second is positive:

$$4\left(-\frac{1}{2}+\frac{3}{5}\right) = 4\left(\frac{-5}{10}+\frac{6}{10}\right)$$

$$= 4\left(\frac{1}{10}\right)$$

Next multiply the result by 4 and simplify the result by putting it in lowest terms:

$$4\left(\frac{1}{10}\right) = \frac{4}{10}$$

$$= \frac{2}{5}$$

4. B: First rewrite the fractions with a common denominator. The lowest common denominator (LCD) of the denominators (15, 20, 5, and 30) is 60. Multiply the numerator and denominator of the each fraction to make their denominators 60:

$$\frac{7}{15}, \frac{9}{20}, \frac{2}{5}, \frac{13}{30} \rightarrow \frac{28}{60}, \frac{27}{60}, \frac{24}{60}, \frac{26}{60}$$

Then put the new list in order from least to greatest by comparing numerators:

$$\frac{28}{60}, \frac{27}{60}, \frac{24}{60}, \frac{26}{60} \rightarrow \frac{24}{60}, \frac{26}{60}, \frac{27}{60}, \frac{28}{60}$$

Finally, change the fractions back to their original forms:

$$\frac{24}{60}, \frac{26}{60}, \frac{27}{60}, \frac{28}{60} \rightarrow \frac{2}{5}, \frac{13}{30}, \frac{9}{20}, \frac{7}{15}$$

5. C: To divide two fractions, invert the second fraction by switching its numerator and denominator:

$$\frac{3}{8} \div \frac{6}{11} = \frac{3}{8} \times \frac{11}{6}$$

Next perform the multiplication to get the answer. Before multiplying the two fractions, cancel any common factors that appear in the numerator of one fraction and the denominator of another to ensure the result is in lowest terms. Here, cancel 3 from the numerator of the first fraction and the denominator of the second:

$$\frac{3}{8} \times \frac{11}{6} = \frac{1}{8} \times \frac{11}{2}$$

Last, multiply the fractions. Multiply the numerators and the denominators separately, and put the products into a new fraction:

$$\frac{1}{8} \times \frac{11}{2} = \frac{11}{16}$$

Computation with Decimal Numbers

1. C: The easiest way to add three numbers is to set up the addition vertically. Line up the decimal points of the three numbers and add, bringing down the decimal point:

$$
\begin{array}{r}
8.31 \\
6.7 \\
+\ 1.889 \\
\hline
16.899
\end{array}
$$

2. B: The easiest way to multiply two numbers is to set up the multiplication vertically. Start by multiplying the numbers normally as if they were whole numbers:

$$
\begin{array}{r}
12.94 \\
\times\ \ 5.8 \\
\hline
10352 \\
+\ 64700 \\
\hline
75052
\end{array}
$$

Next you need to decide where to put the decimal point in the answer. In the original numbers, 12.94 and 5.8, the first number has two digits after the decimal point, and the second has just one. Therefore, you should place the decimal point three places from the rightmost digit of the product. The correct answer is 75.052.

3. A: The tenths place is the first digit after the decimal. In this case, it is a 5. To round to the nearest tenth, the given number will either be rounded down to 94.5 or rounded up to 94.6. To determine which way to round, look at the digit after the 5 (the hundredths place), which is a 4. Since this number is less than five, round down. Therefore, the correct answer is 94.5.

4. C: Since the problem involves multiplying three quantities together, you could multiply from left-to-right. However, a much easier way to solve the problem is to realize that one of the quantities is zero. The product of zero and any other number is zero, thus the answer must be zero.

5. A: The easiest way to subtract two decimals is to set up the subtraction vertically. Rewrite each number so that they all have the same number of digits after the decimal. Then subtract vertically:

$$
\begin{array}{r}
14.320 \\
-\ 12.915 \\
\hline
1.405
\end{array}
$$

Problems involving Percents

1. D: First convert the percent to a decimal number by dividing it by 100, or, equivalently, by moving the decimal point two places to the left:

$$56\% = 0.56$$

Next, calculate 56% of 25 by multiplying 25 by 0.56:

$$0.56 \times 25 = 14$$

2. B: A percent can be converted to a fraction by putting it over 100, then reducing to lowest terms by finding the greatest common factor (GCF) of the numerator and denominator:

$$45\% = \frac{45}{100} = \frac{9}{20}$$

3. C: A percent is a part divided by the whole ($\frac{part}{whole}$). In this problem, the part is 42 and the whole is 56, so the percent can be expressed as $\frac{42}{56}$, or .075:

$$\frac{42}{56} = 42 \div 56$$

$$= 0.75$$

Convert the decimal to a percent by multiplying it by 100 (or equivalently by moving the decimal point two places to the right) and adding a percent sign:
$$0.75 = 75\%$$

4. C: First add the numbers of boys and girls to find the total number of students:

$$48 + 72 = 120$$

Use this total to find the percent of the students that are boys. You can think of percents as a part divided by the whole ($\frac{part}{whole}$). The part is the number of boys, 48, and the whole is the total number of students, 120. Next convert the fraction $\frac{48}{120}$ to a decimal. Divide the numerator by the denominator to get a decimal number:

$$\frac{48}{120} = 48 \div 120$$

$$= 0.4$$

Last, convert the decimal to a percent by multiplying it by 100 (or equivalently by moving the decimal point two places to the right) and adding a percent sign:

$$0.4 = 40\%$$

5. A: Since the percent is given as a fraction, the first step will be to convert it to a decimal (but one that is still a percent):

$$\frac{1}{2}\% = 0.5\%$$

Convert the percent to a proper decimal number by dividing it by 100, or, equivalently, by moving the decimal point two places to the left:

$$0.5\% = 0.005$$

Finally, calculate 0.5% of 40 by multiplying 40 by 0.005:

$$0.005 \times 40 = 0.2$$

Estimation, Ordering, Number Sense

1. C: A perfect square is a positive integer that can be written as the square of another number. For instance, 16 and 100 are both perfect squares since $4^2 = 16$ and $10^2 = 100$. This problem asks for an estimate of the square root. The answer choice that when squared is closest to 82 is 9 since $9^2 = 81$.

2. D: To begin, round each number to its first decimal place:

$$80{,}389 \times 597.39 \approx 80{,}000 \times 600$$

Now multiply the rounded numbers. Multiplying numbers with a lot of zeroes can be done quickly even if the numbers are very large. First multiply the numbers without the zeroes:
$$8 \times 6 = 48$$

Next, add the zeroes that were removed. Since 80,000 has four zeroes and 600 has two, add six zeroes to the right side (4 + 2 = 6) to obtain the final result:

$$80{,}000 \times 600 = 48{,}000{,}000$$

3. A: Since the numbers provided are a fraction and three decimal numbers, it will be easier to compare these numbers by converting the fraction to a decimal:

$$\frac{8}{5} = 8 \div 5$$

$$= 1.6$$

The list now consists of 1.71, 1.6, −2, and 1.685. Since −2 is negative and the other numbers are positive, −2 must be the smallest of the four.

The remaining numbers are 1.71, 1.6 and 1.685 (or 1.710, 1.600, and 1.685). They all have a 1 in the ones place, so the ones place is inconclusive. Comparing the digits in the tenths place shows that 1.6 and 1.685 are both smaller than 1.71. Finally, comparing the hundredths place shows that 1.6 (or 1.600) is smaller than 1.695. Therefore, from least to greatest, the order of the numbers is as follows:

$$-2, 1.6, 1.685, 1.71 \quad \text{or} \quad -2, \frac{8}{5}, 1.685, 1.71$$

4. C: Since 47 is just a little more than 45, the first fraction, $\frac{47}{45}$, is a little more than 1. Similarly, 20 is a little less than 21, the second fraction, $\frac{20}{21}$, is a little less than 1. Therefore, when you add them up, the result will be very close to 2.

5. D: The greatest number is found by estimating each answer choice.

A) In choice A, the percent is about 25%, which is equal to one-fourth. One-fourth of 120 is 30. So, 24.1% of 120 is about 30.

B) In choice B, the second number is close to 100. If you take any percent of 100, the result is the original percent. For instance, 81% of 100 is equal to 81. Therefore, 34.2% of 99 is about 34.

C) In choice C, the percent is about 50%, which is equal to one-half. One-half of 72 is 36. So, 49.4% of 72 is about 36.

D) In choice D, the percent is also about 50. One-half of 90 is 45. So, 51.1% of 90 is about 45.

Since 45 is much larger than the other estimations, the best answer is choice D.

Word Problems and Applications

1. C: The problem states that three-fifths of the 300 students are girls, so calculate the product of three-fifths $\left(\frac{3}{5}\right)$ and 300:

$$\frac{3}{5} \cdot an = \frac{3}{5} \cdot \frac{300}{1}$$

$$= \frac{3}{1} \cdot \frac{60}{1}$$

$$= 180$$

2. A: First add the cost of the three items together:

2.55
3.79

$$\frac{+\ 3.09}{9.43}$$

Subtract this amount from $20.00 to find the change:

$$\frac{\begin{array}{r} 20.00 \\ -\ \ 9.43 \end{array}}{10.57}$$

3. A: First calculate the dollar value of the sales tax. To find this value, multiply $25,000 by 0.05:

$$0.05 \cdot \$25,000 = \$1,250$$

To find the total cost of the car with sales tax, add the sales tax to the original price of the car:

$$\$25,000 + \$1,250 = \$26,250$$

4. B: First add the number of boys and girls to find the total number of students in the school:

$$270 + 450 = 720$$

Next, divide the number of boys, 270, by 720 and convert the result to a percent:

$$\begin{aligned} 270 \div 720 &= 0.375 \\ &= 37.5\% \end{aligned}$$

5. D: Find the total revenue by multiplying the number of computers by the price of each computer. Since the question uses the word "approximately", estimate this amount by first rounding the numbers:

$$810,602 \approx 800,000$$

$$\$895 \approx \$900$$

Then multiply the rounded numbers:

$$800,000 \cdot \$900 = \$720,000,000$$

Therefore, the total revenue was about $720 million.

Elementary Algebra

Real Numbers

1. D: The set of real numbers is comprised of two main types of numbers: rational numbers and irrational numbers. A rational numbers is a number that can be written as a fraction. Integers, fractions, and repeating or terminating decimal numbers are all rational numbers since they can all be written as fractions. Irrational numbers, on the other hand, are numbers that cannot be written as fractions.

Look at the given choices starting with choice A and determine one which is irrational. Choice A is a rational number since $-5 = -\frac{5}{1}$. Choice B is given in fractional form already so it is rational as well. Choice C is a repeating decimal equal to $\frac{1}{3}$ so it is rational. Choice D, however, is π (the Greek letter "pi"), the symbol for a specific decimal number (approximately 3.1416) that goes on forever without repeating. Thus, it is the only irrational number among the choices.

2. C: First simplify the expression in parentheses. To subtract two fractions, rewrite them with a common denominator and then subtract the numerators:

$$\left(\frac{2}{3} - \frac{1}{4}\right) \div \frac{1}{4} = \left(\frac{8}{12} - \frac{3}{12}\right) \div \frac{1}{4}$$

$$= \frac{5}{12} \div \frac{1}{4}$$

Now divide the fractions. Invert the second fraction by switching its numerator and denominator and change the operation to multiplication. Cancel any common factors that appear in the numerator of one fraction and the denominator of another to simplify the multiplication:

$$\frac{5}{12} \div \frac{1}{4} = \frac{5}{12} \times \frac{4}{1}$$

$$= \frac{5}{3} \times \frac{1}{1}$$

$$= \frac{5}{3}$$

3. C: First simplify the numerator and the denominator:

$$\frac{4.8 - 12.3}{-1 - 4} = \frac{-7.5}{-5}$$

Next, simplify the resulting fraction by dividing:

$$\frac{-7.5}{-5} = -7.5 \div (-5)$$
$$= 1.5$$

4. A: Evaluate a square root by first factoring the radicand (the number under the radical sign) by taking out the greatest perfect square that divides it evenly. In this problem, the radicand is 63, whose greatest perfect square factor is 9. Next rewrite the result as the product of two radicals:

$$\sqrt{63} = \sqrt{9 \times 7}$$
$$= \sqrt{9} \times \sqrt{7}$$

Finally, finish simplifying the result using the fact that $\sqrt{9} = 3$:

$$\sqrt{9} \times \sqrt{7} = 3\sqrt{7}$$

5. B: Multiply square root radicals by multiplying the radicands (the numbers under the radical sign) and putting the result under a square root sign:

$$\sqrt{3} \times \sqrt{7} = \sqrt{3 \times 7}$$
$$= \sqrt{21}$$

Linear Equations, Inequalities and Systems

1. A: First simplify the left side of the equation by distributing the -4 and then adding the constants together:

$$2 - 4(x + 3) = 6$$
$$2 - 4x - 12 = 6$$
$$-4x - 10 = 6$$

Next isolate the variable x by adding 10 to both sides. Last, divide both sides by the coefficient of x, -4, to solve the equation:

$$-4x = 16$$
$$x = -4$$

2. B: First simplify the right side of the equation by combining like terms:

$$3a = 2a + a + 4a - 4$$

$$3a = 7a - 4$$

Next, subtract $3a$ and add 4 to both sides of the equation to isolate the variable on the right side. Finally, solve the resulting equation by dividing both sides by the coefficient of a, 4:

$$3a = 7a - 4$$

$$0 = 4a - 4$$

$$4 = 4a$$

$$1 = a$$

3. B: Inequalities are solved in much the same way as equations. The only difference is that if multiplying or dividing both sides by a negative number, the inequality sign must be flipped (i.e. > becomes <, ≥ becomes ≤.) Begin by isolating the variable y by subtracting 4 from both sides:

$$4 - \frac{1}{3}y > 5$$

$$-\frac{1}{3}y > 1$$

Then solve the resulting inequality by multiplying both sides by -3 to get rid of the coefficient of y. Since this involves multiplying both sides of the inequality by a negative number, flip the inequality sign as well:

$$y < -3$$

4. A: The given equations form a system of linear equations. Since one equation has x and the other has $-x$, the elimination method is a good choice. First add the equations together to eliminate the variable x:

$$x + 3y = 3$$
$$\underline{-x + y = 5}$$
$$4y = 8$$

Then solve the resulting equation for y by dividing both sides by 4:

$$y = 2$$

Finally, to calculate the value of x, substitute 2 for y into one of the equations and solve for x:

$$x + 3(2) = 3$$

$$x + 6 = 3$$

$$x = -3$$

5. C: The given equations form a system of linear equations. Since the first equation is already given in terms of x, it will be easier to solve it using the substitution method. Start by substituting $2y - 3$ for x in the second equation:

$$2x + \frac{1}{2}y = 3$$

$$2(2y - 3) + \frac{1}{2}y = 3$$

Next, solve the resulting equation for y. Distribute the 2 and then combine like y-terms in the result:

$$4y - 6 + \frac{1}{2}y = 3$$

$$\frac{9}{2}y - 6 = 3$$

Finally, isolate the variable y by adding 6 to both sides and then dividing both sides by the coefficient of y, which is $\frac{9}{2}$ (or, equivalently, multiply by 2 and divide by 9):

$$\frac{9}{2}y = 9$$

$$y = 2$$

Quadratic Expressions and Equations

1. A: To add quadratic expressions, combine like terms. In this problem, there are three sets of like terms: the y^2-terms, the y-terms, and the constants. Set up the addition vertically, making sure to line up like terms, and then add them together:

$$\begin{array}{r} y^2 + 9y - 2 \\ + \ 4y^2 - y - 5 \\ \hline 5y^2 + 8y - 7 \end{array}$$

2. D: To multiply two binomials, use FOIL. FOIL is an acronym that stands for "First, Outer, Inner, Last." Multiply the first terms of the binomial, then the outer terms of the binomials, then the inner terms of the binomials, and finally the last terms of the binomials:

Multiply the First terms of $(x + 3)(x - 1)$: $x \cdot x = x^2$
Multiply the Outer terms of $(x + 3)(x - 1)$: $x \cdot (-1) = -x$
Multiply the Inner terms of $(x + 3)(x - 1)$: $3 \cdot x = 3x$
Multiply the Last terms of $(x + 3)(x - 1)$: $3 \cdot (-1) = -3$

Next, add the products and simplify the result by combining like terms:

$$(x + 3)(x - 1) = x^2 - x + 3x - 3$$

$$= x^2 + 2x - 3$$

3. D: Simplify the expression by pulling out the greatest common factor between the two terms, which is 2:

$$2c^2 - 32 = 2(c^2 - 16)$$

Next, factor the expression in parentheses. Since c^2 is the square of c and 16 is the square of 4, $c^2 - 16$ is the difference of two squares. Therefore, it can be factored as $a^2 - b^2 = (a - b)(a + b)$. For this problem, use the values $a = c$ and $b = 4$:

$$2(c^2 - 16 = 2(c - 4)(c + 4)$$

4. B: The given equation is a quadratic equation that can be solved by factorization. First, move everything to one side to get it in the correct form, by subtracting 6 from both sides:

$$x^2 + 5x = 6$$

$$x^2 + 5x - 6 = 0$$

Since the left side expression is a trinomial in the form $ax^2 + bx + c$ with $a = 1$, the factorization will be a product of two binomials in the form $(x + a)(x + b)$. The values of a and b are two numbers that add up to 5 and have a product of -6. The only numbers that satisfy these requirements are 1 and -6. Substitute these values into $(x + a)(x + b)$ to get the factorization of the trinomial:

$$x^2 + 5x - 6 = 0$$

$$(x - 1)(x + 6) = 0$$

Finally, use the zero-product rule to solve for x. The zero-product rule states that if the product of two expressions is zero, then one of the expressions must be zero. For this problem that means that either $x + 1$ is zero or $x - 6$ is zero. Set each factor to zero and solve for x:

$$x - 1 = 0 \quad \text{or} \quad x + 6 = 0$$

$$x = 1 \qquad\qquad x = -6$$

Therefore, the solutions to the equation are $x = 1$ and $x = -6$.

5. B: The given equation is a quadratic equation that can be solved by factoring. Since it is a trinomial in the form $ax^2 + bx + c$ with $a > 1$, the factorization will be a product of two binomials in the form $(ax + b)(cx + d)$. Use trial-and-error to find the correct values of a, b, c, and d. In this case, the values of a and c must multiply to 2 (the coefficient of the n^2-term), so they must be 1 and 2; the values of b and d must multiply to 4 (the coefficient), so they can either be 1 and 4 or 2 and 2. Try different combinations until finding the correct n-term. For instance, the following combination does not work because the n-term comes out to $6n$, instead of $9n$:

$$(n + 1)(2n + 4) = 2n^2 + 4n + 2n + 4$$

$$= 2n^2 + 6n + 4$$

The following is the correct factorization:

$$2n^2 + 9n + 4 = 0$$

$$(n + 4)(2n + 1) = 0$$

Next solve for n by using the zero-product rule. The zero-product rule states that if the product of two expressions is zero, then one of the expressions must be zero. For this problem that means that either $2n + 1$ is zero or $n + 4$ is zero. Set each factor to zero and solve for n:

$$n + 4 = 0 \quad \text{or} \quad 2n + 1 = 0$$

$$n = -4 \qquad\qquad n = -\frac{1}{2}$$

Therefore, the solutions to the equation are $n = -4$ and $= -\frac{1}{2}$.

Algebraic Expressions and Equations

1. B: To evaluate the expression for the given values of x and y, substitute the values into the expression and then calculate the result:

$$2x^2 + 5x - y^2 = 2(3)^2 + 5(3) - (5)^2$$

$$= 2 \cdot 9 + 5 \cdot 3 - 25$$

$$= 18 + 15 - 25$$

$$= 8$$

2. B: A solution satisfies an equation if it makes the equation true. Substitute each x-value into the equation to see if the result is a true equality. Start with choice A, $x = 2$:

$$5x = 15$$

$$5(2) = 15$$

$$10 = 15$$

Since the resulting equation is false, $x = 2$ does not satisfy the given equation. Next try choice B, $x = 3$:

$$5x = 15$$

$$5(3) = 15$$

$$15 = 15$$

Since the resulting equation is true, $x = 3$ satisfies the given equation.

3. B: To divide expressions that contain variables, divide pairs of like variables (or constants) that appear in both the numerator and denominator. For this problem, first divide the constants: $12 \div 3$, then divide the a's: $a^2 \div a$. Since $a^2 \div a$ is equivalent to $\frac{a^2}{a^1}$, use the quotient rule, $\frac{x^a}{x^b} = x^{a-b}$, to simplify it. There is no change to b since the divisor does not contain the variable b :

$$\frac{12a^2 b}{3a} = \frac{4a^{2-1}b}{1}$$

$$= 4ab$$

4. D: The quickest method to evaluate this expression is to distribute the exponent of 2 to each of the values inside the parenthesis using the rule $(x^a)^b = x^{a \cdot b}$:

$$(4x^5)^2 = 4^2 \cdot x^{5 \cdot 2}$$

$$= 16x^{10}$$

5. A: To simplify the given expression, start by distributing the 3 across $(2y - x)$:

$$4x + 3(2y - x) = 4x + 3 \cdot 2y + 3 \cdot (-x)$$

$$= 4x + 6y - 3x$$

There are two x-terms in the resulting expression, $4x$ and $-3x$. Combine them by adding their coefficients:

$$4x + 6y - 3x = 1x + 6y$$

$$= x + 6y$$

Word Problems and Applications

1. C: The volume of the box is the product of $\sqrt{3}$, $2\sqrt{5}$, and 4. To multiply two or more square root radicals, multiply the coefficients and then multiply the radicands:

$$\sqrt{3} \times 2\sqrt{5} \times 4 = 2\sqrt{15} \times 4$$

$$= 8\sqrt{15}$$

2. D: The cost of the cab ride is $3.60 plus $0.75 times the distance, excluding the first half-mile. This is given by the expression $3.60 + 0.75(d - 0.5)$.

3. D: First create variables for the two unknowns in the problem. Let d represent the number of dimes and q represent the number of quarters. Given that Adam has 24 coins and that the coins are worth $3.30 altogether, a system of linear equations can be defined:

$$d + q = 24$$

$$10d + 24q = 330$$

Solve this system of equations using the elimination method. To eliminate q, multiply the first equation by 25, and then subtract the equations from one another:

$$25(d + q = 24)$$
$$10 + 25q = 330$$

$\rightarrow$

$$25d + 25q = 600$$
$$-(10d + 25q = 330)$$
$$\overline{15d + 0\ \ = 270}$$

Finally, solve the resulting equation by dividing both sides by 15. The result is $d = 18$, which means that Adam has 18 dimes.

4. A: First establish a variable, s, for the length of the smaller square. Since the larger square is 3 feet longer than the smaller one, its length is $s + 3$. Given that the difference between the areas of the two squares is 75, and the area of any square is equal to its side lengths squared, the following equation can be established:

$$(s + 3)^2 - s^2 = 75$$

Simplify the left side of the equation:

$$(s + 3)^2 - s^2 = 75$$

$$(s + 3)(s + 3) - s^2 = 75$$

$$s^2 + 6s + 9 - s^2 = 75$$

$$6s + 9 = 75$$

Isolate the variable and divide both sides by its coefficient to solve for s:

$$6s = 66$$

$$s = 11$$

Therefore, the length of the smaller square is 11 feet.

5. C: The ball will hit the ground when its height is zero. In mathematical notation, this will happen when the expression for its height is equal to zero:

$$-16t^2 + 47t + 3 = 0$$

To solve this equation, factor the expression on the left side of the equation and then use the zero-product rule:

$$(-t + 3)(16t + 1) = 0$$

$$-t + 3 = 0 \quad \text{or} \quad 16t + 1 = 0$$

$$t = 3 \qquad\qquad t = -\frac{1}{16}$$

The answer only makes sense when t is positive, so discard the negative value. Thus, the ball will hit the ground exactly 3 seconds after it is thrown.

College Level Mathematics

Algebraic Operations

1. D: The given expression is a trinomial that can be factored. Since the expression is a trinomial of degree 4 (not 2), create a temporary variable, u, to put it in quadratic form and eventually factor it. Letting $u = y^2$, substitute u for every occurrence of y^2 in the given expression:

$$y^4 + 3y^2 - 4 = (y^2)^2 + 3(y^2) - 4$$

$$= u^2 + 3u - 4$$

Next, factor the resulting expression:

$$u^2 + 3u - 4 = (u + 4)(u - 1)$$

Since u was only a temporary variable created to make the problem easier, substitute y^2 back in the expression:

$$(u + 4)(u - 1) = (y^2 + 4)(y^2 - 1)$$

This is a valid factorization for the original expression. However, it can be factored further since $y^2 - 1$ is the difference of two squares:

$$(y^2 + 4)(y^2 - 1) = (y^2 + 4)(y - 1)(y + 1)$$

2. C: To simplify the expression, start by factoring the numerator and denominator. For the numerator, find two numbers whose sum is −3 and whose product is −10, and then put those numbers into the form $(x + a)(x + b)$. For the denominator, factor out the greatest common factor (GCF), which is 4:

$$\frac{x^2-3x-10}{4x-20} = \frac{(x-5)(x+2)}{4(x-5)}$$

Last, simplify the expression by cancelling out the common factor of $(x - 5)$:

$$\frac{(x-5)(x+2)}{4(x-5)} = \frac{x+2}{4}$$

3. D: First use the definition of an exponent to rewrite the given expression as the product of two trinomials:

$$(2n^2 + 3n + 1)^2 = (2n^2 + 3n + 1)(2n^2 + 3n + 1)$$

Next, multiply each term in the first trinomial by the second trinomial (in its entirety):

$$(2n^2 + 3n + 1)(2n^2 + 3n + 1) =$$

$$2n^2(2n^2 + 3n + 1) + 3n(2n^2 + 3n + 1) + 1(2n^2 + 3n + 1)$$

Finally, distribute the three products and combine like terms in the result:

$$2n^2(2n^2 + 3n + 1) + 3n(2n^2 + 3n + 1) + 1(2n^2 + 3n + 1)$$

$$= (4n^4 + 6n^3 + 2n^2) + (6n^3 + 9n^2 + 3n) + (2n^2 + 3n + 1)$$

$$= 4n^4 + 12n^3 + 13n^2 + 6n + 1$$

4. B: Raising a number or an expression to a negative power is the same thing as raising it to a positive power and then taking the reciprocal of the result. As a result, the given expression is equal to the reciprocal of $(4a)^2$:

$$(4a)^{-2} = \frac{1}{(4a)^2}$$

Simplify the denominator in this expression by distributing the now-positive exponent:

$$\frac{1}{(4a)^2} = \frac{1}{16a^2}$$

5. C: Exponential expressions can only be subtracted if they have the same base and exponent (and only differ in coefficients.) The given terms have the same base but not the same exponent. The difference between the exponents is $\frac{5}{2} - \frac{3}{2} = 1$.

Therefore, taking out a 3 (thus reducing the exponent by 1) from the first term will make the remaining values like terms that can then be combined:

$$3^{\frac{5}{2}} - 3^{\frac{3}{2}} = 3 \cdot 3^{\frac{3}{2}} - 1 \cdot 3^{\frac{3}{2}}$$

$$= (3-1) \cdot 3^{\frac{3}{2}}$$

$$= 2 \cdot 3^{\frac{3}{2}}$$

The result can now be written as a radical expression with no exponents. Start by taking out another 3 from $3^{\frac{3}{2}}$:

$$2 \cdot 3^{\frac{3}{2}} = 2 \cdot 3 \cdot 3^{\frac{1}{2}}$$

$$= 6 \cdot 3^{\frac{1}{2}}$$

Last, use the rule $a^{\frac{m}{n}} = \left(\sqrt[n]{a}\right)^m = \sqrt[n]{a^m}$ to rewrite the exponent as a square root:

$$6 \cdot 3^{\frac{1}{2}} = 6\sqrt{3}$$

Solutions of Equations and Inequalities

1. D: Start by rewriting the equation in the form $ax^2 + bx + c = 0$ by subtracting 1 from both sides:

$$4x^2 + 2x = 1$$

$$4x^2 + 2x - 1 = 0$$

The left side cannot be factored, so use the quadratic formula. For the variables in the quadratic formula, use a = 4, b = 2, and c = −1:

$$x = \frac{-b \pm \sqrt{b^2 - 4ac}}{2a}$$

$$= \frac{-(2) \pm \sqrt{(2)^2 - 4(4)(-1)}}{2(4)}$$

$$= \frac{-2 \pm \sqrt{4+16}}{8}$$

$$= \frac{-2 \pm \sqrt{20}}{8}$$

$$= \frac{-2 \pm 2\sqrt{5}}{8}$$

$$= -\frac{1}{4} \pm \frac{\sqrt{5}}{4}$$

2. B: Solve the inequality by changing the inequality sign to an equal sign and solve the resulting equation by factoring the left side:

$$x^2 - 7x + 10 = 0$$

$$(x - 2)(x - 5) = 0$$

$$x - 2 = 0 \quad \text{or} \quad x - 5 = 0$$

$$x = 2 \qquad\qquad x = 5$$

Since the original inequality sign was a greater-than-or-equal-to sign (rather than just a greater-than sign), the solution set will include $x = 2$ and $x = 5$.

These two solutions divide the number line into three distinct regions: $x < 2$, $2 < x < 5$, and $x > 5$. To see which regions are in the solution set, pick one test value from each region and substitute it in the original inequality. If the result is a true inequality, then the whole region is part of the solution set. Otherwise, the whole region is not part in the solution set:

Region	Test Value	$x^2 - 7x + 10 \geq 0$	Conclusion
$x < 2$	0	$(0)^2 - 7(0) + 10 \geq 0$ $10 \geq 0$	Part of the solution set
$2 < x < 5$	3	$(3)^2 - 7(3) + 10 \geq 0$ $9 - 21 + 10 \geq 0$ $-2 \geq 0$	Not part of the solution set
$x > 5$	6	$(6)^2 - 7(6) + 10 \geq 0$ $36 - 42 + 10 \geq 0$ $4 \geq 0$	Part of the solution set

- 87 -

Therefore, the solution set is $x \leq 2$ or $x \geq 5$.

3. A: The given equations form a system of three linear equation with three variables x, y, and z. Organize the equations by writing them vertically with the corresponding variables lined up:

$$
\begin{array}{ll}
(1) & x + 2y = 1 \\
(2) & 3y + z = 1 \\
(3) & {-x} + y + 3z = 8
\end{array}
$$

Now solve the system using the elimination method. Since equation (1) has an x and equation (2) has a $-x$, add them to eliminate x. The result is a new equation, equation (4), which only has y and z for variables:

$$
\begin{array}{ll}
(1) & x + 2y = 1 \\
(3) & \underline{{-x} + y + 3z = 8} \\
(4) & 3y + 3z = 9
\end{array}
$$

Next subtract equation (2) from equation (4) to eliminate y:

$$
\begin{array}{ll}
(4) & 3y + 3z = 9 \\
(2) & \underline{-(3y + z) = -1} \\
(5) & 2z = 8
\end{array}
$$

If you solve the resulting equation for z, you get the value $z = 4$. Use this value to calculate the value of y since the value of x cannot be determined from z. Start by substituting 4 for z in equation (2) and solve for y:

$$
\begin{array}{ll}
(2) & 3y + (4) = 1 \\
& 3y = -3 \\
& y = -1
\end{array}
$$

Finally, substitute -1 for y in equation (1) and solve the resulting equation for x.

$$
\begin{array}{ll}
(1) & x + 2y = 1 \\
& x + 2(-1) = 1 \\
& x = 3
\end{array}
$$

4. D: To solve the equation, first get rid of the denominators by multiplying both sides of the equation by $x(x - 3)$ and simplifying the result:

$$
\frac{4}{x-3} - \frac{2}{x} = 1
$$

$$x(x-3)\left[\frac{4}{x-3} - \frac{2}{x}\right] = x(x-3)\cdot 1$$

$$4x - 2(x-3) = x(x-3)$$

$$4x - 2x + 6 = x^2 - 3x$$

$$2x + 6 = x^2 - 3x$$

The result is a quadratic equation. Move everything to one side and then solve for x by factoring the left side and applying the zero-product rule:

$$x^2 - 5x - 6 = 0$$

$$(x+1)(x-6) = 0$$

$$x + 1 = 0 \quad \text{or} \quad x - 6 = 0$$

$$x = -1 \qquad\qquad x = 6$$

Therefore, the possible solutions are $x = -1$ and $x = 6$. Since neither of these values will cause division by zero when substituted back into the original equation, they are both valid solutions.

5. B: Start by squaring both sides of the equation and simplifying the result:

$$\left(\sqrt{3x-2}\right)^2 = (x-2)^2$$

$$3x - 2 = x^2 - 4x + 4$$

Next, move everything to one side and factor to find solutions for x:

$$x^2 - 7x + 6 = 0$$

$$(x-1)(x-6) = 0$$

$$x - 1 = 0 \quad \text{or} \quad x - 6 = 0$$

$$x = 1 \qquad\qquad x = 6$$

Therefore, the possible solutions are $x = 1$ and $x = 6$. Substitute these solutions into the original equation to see if they are valid solutions:

$$\sqrt{3x - 2} = x - 2 \qquad\qquad \sqrt{3x - 2} = x - 2$$
$$\sqrt{3(1) - 2} = (1) - 2 \qquad \sqrt{3(6) - 2} = (6) - 2$$
$$\sqrt{1} = 1 - 2 \qquad\qquad \sqrt{16} = 6 - 2$$
$$1 = 1 - 2 \; \textit{False} \qquad\qquad 4 = 6 - 2 \; \textit{True}$$

Since only $x = 6$ leads to a true equality, that is the only solution.

Coordinate Geometry

1. A: The coordinates of a point are an ordered pair (x, y) that indicate where the point is located on the coordinate plane. Find the coordinates by determining the distance each point is from both the x and y axes. The leftmost point is 1 unit to the left of the y-axis and sits on the x-axis. Therefore, its coordinates are $(-1, 0)$. The top point is 2 units to the right of the y-axis and 4 units above the x-axis, or $(2, 4)$. The bottom point is 2 units to the right of the y-axis and 2 units below the x-axis, of $(2, -2)$.

2. A: The equation of line L is given in slope-intercept form $y = mx + b$, therefore the slope of line L is $m = 3$, while its y-intercept is $b = 1$.

Two lines are perpendicular if their slopes are negative reciprocals. Since the slope of line L is 3, the slope of a line perpendicular to it must be $= -\frac{1}{3}$. Substitute this value into the general slope-intercept form $y = mx + b$ to find an equation for any perpendicular to L:

$$y = -\frac{1}{3}x + b$$

Since the point $(-3, -5)$ must be intersected by the perpendicular line, and is thus a point on that line, substitute $x = -3$ and $y = -5$ into the equation above and then solve for b:

$$(-5) = -\frac{1}{3}(-3) + b$$
$$-5 = 1 + b$$
$$-6 = b$$

Finally, plug this value for b into the equation $y = -\frac{1}{3}x + b$ to obtain the solution:

$$y = -\frac{1}{3}x - 6$$

3. A: A conic section is a curve obtained by the intersection of a cone and a plane. The four conic sections are the circle, the ellipse, the parabola, and the hyperbola. The following chart shows a general equation for each of the four conic sections:

Conic Section	Equation
Circle	$(x - h)^2 + (y - k)^2 = r^2$
Ellipse	$\frac{(x-h)^2}{a^2} + \frac{(y-k)^2}{b^2} = 1$
Parabola	$(x - h)^2 = 4a(y - k)$
Hyperbola	$\frac{(x-h)^2}{a^2} - \frac{(y-k)^2}{b^2} = 1$

The given equation can be rewritten as $(x - 0)^2 + (y - 0)^2 = (\sqrt{11})^2$, thus it is the equation of a circle.

4. B: The graph of a quadratic equation is a parabola, a U-shaped curve, which is also one of the four conic sections. To graph the given equation, substitute three or more values of x into the given equation and then calculate the corresponding values of y. The results are shown in the table of values below:

x	$y = x^2 + 2x - 1$	(x,y)
−2	$(-2)^2 + 2(-2) - 1 = -1$	$(-2,-1)$
−1	$(-1)^2 + 2(-1) - 1 = -2$	$(-1,-2)$
0	$(0)^2 + 2(0) - 1 = -1$	$(0,-1)$
1	$(1)^2 + 2(1) - 1 = 2$	$(1,2)$
2	$(2)^2 + 2(2) - 1 = 7$	$(2,7)$

From the table, the graph of the equation must pass through the points, $(-2,-1)$, $(-1,-2)$, $(0,-1)$, $(1,2)$, and $(2,7)$. Graph these points on a coordinate plane and then connect them with a parabola line. This result matches graph B:

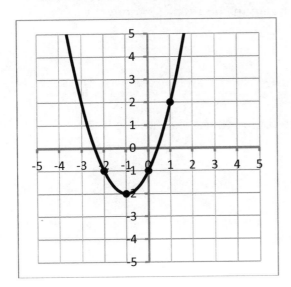

5. D: To graph an inequality, first graph its boundary line(s). Change the inequality sign to an equal sign and graph the resulting equation, $y = 3x + 1$. Since the given inequality is a less-than-or-equal-to sign graph it using a solid line (rather than a dotted one):

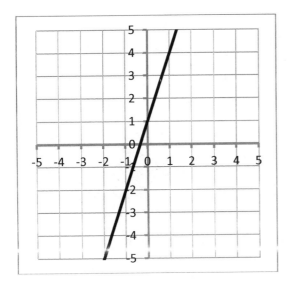

Next, to determine which region to shade, choose a test point in one of the regions. The easiest point to test is the origin (0, 0). Substitute $x = 0$ and $y = 0$ into the given inequality; if the result is a true inequality, then the whole region that contains the origin should be shaded, otherwise, the other region should be shaded:

$$y \leq 3x + 1$$
$$0 \leq 3(0) + 1$$
$$0 \leq 1$$

Since the result is a true inequality, shade the region to the right of the line:

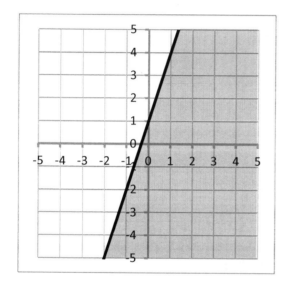

Applications and Other Algebra Topics

1. C: Start by rewriting the equation in the form $ax^2 + bx + c = 0$. Distribute the left side and then move everything to one side:

$$2x(x + 1) = -3$$

$$2x^2 + 2x = -3$$

$$2x^2 + 2x + 3 = 0$$

Since the left side cannot be factored, use the quadratic formula to solve the equation. For the variables in the quadratic formula, use $a = 2$, $b = 2$, and $c = 3$:

$$x = \frac{-b \pm \sqrt{b^2 - 4ac}}{2a}$$

$$= \frac{-(2) \pm \sqrt{(2)^2 - 4(2)(3)}}{2(2)}$$

$$= \frac{-2 \pm \sqrt{-20}}{4}$$

The result contains the square root of a negative number, so the solution is not a real number. Instead, it is a complex number that contains the imaginary number i, which is the square root of -1:

$$x = \frac{-2 \pm \sqrt{-1} \times \sqrt{20}}{4}$$

$$= \frac{-2 \pm 2i\sqrt{5}}{4}$$

$$= -\frac{1}{2} \pm \frac{i\sqrt{5}}{2}$$

2. D: Each term in the sequence is 3 more than the last. Therefore, this sequence is an arithmetic sequence with a common difference d of 3.

To find the sum of the first 20 terms of the sequence, begin by calculating the first term, a_1, as well as the 20th term, a_{20}, of the given sequence. The first term is given in the problem. Its value is $a_1 = 2$. The 20th term, however, must be found by using the formula for the nth term of an arithmetic sequence:

$$a_n = a_1 + (n - 1)d$$

Substitute the values $n = 20$, $a_1 = 2$, and $d = 3$ into this formula and then simplify the result:

$$a_{20} = 2 + (20 - 1) \cdot 3$$

$$= 2 + 19 \cdot 3$$

$$= 59$$

Therefore, the 20th term in the sequence is 59. Next solve the problem by using the formula for the sum of the first n terms of an arithmetic sequence:

$$S_n = \frac{n}{2}(a_1 + a_n)$$

Substitute the values $n = 20$, $a_1 = 2$, and $a_{20} = 59$ into the formula and then simplify the result:

$$
\begin{aligned}
S_{20} &= \frac{20}{2}(2 + 59) \\
&= 10 \cdot 61 \\
&= 610
\end{aligned}
$$

3. D: The number of bacteria in the Petri dish doubles every day, so the first four days are:

Day	1	2	3	4
Number of Bacteria	500	1000	2000	4000

The number of bacteria forms a sequence in which each term is two times the last. Therefore, this sequence is a geometric sequence with a common ratio r of 2. Calculate the 14th term of the sequence using the formula for the nth term of the geometric term:
$$a_n = a_1 r^{n-1}$$

Substitute the values $n = 14$, $a_1 = 500$, and $r = 2$ into the formula and then simplify the result:

$$
\begin{aligned}
a_{14} &= 500 \cdot 2^{14-1} \\
&= 500 \cdot 2^{13} \\
&= 500 \cdot 8{,}192 \\
&= 409{,}600
\end{aligned}
$$

Therefore, the Petri dish will contain 409,600 bacteria after 14 days.

4. B: A permutation is an arrangement of a set of objects in which the order of the objects does matter. The notation $_nP_k$ gives the number of different permutation you can make if you use a total of n objects to form a group of k objects without using an object more than once. The value of $_nP_k$ can be found using the formula below:

$$_nP_k = \frac{n!}{(n-k)!}$$

In this problem, the committee is electing four people for four separate positions from a pool of 12 people. Thus, to find the number of possible outcomes, calculate $_{12}P_4$:

$$\begin{aligned}
_{12}P_4 &= \frac{12!}{(12-4)!} \\
&= \frac{12 \times 11 \times ... \times 1}{8 \times 7 \times ... \times 1} \\
&= \frac{12 \times 11 \times 10 \times 9}{1} \\
&= 11,880
\end{aligned}$$

Therefore, there are 11,880 ways that the committee can elect the four positions.

5. A: A. combination is an arrangement of a set of objects in which the order of the objects does not matter. The notation $\binom{n}{k}$ gives the number of different combinations you can make if you use a total of n objects to form a group of k objects without using an object more than once. The value of $\binom{n}{k}$ can be found using the formula below:

$$\binom{n}{k} = \frac{n!}{k!(n-k)!}$$

This problem wants the total number of five-card hands that are only spades. Two hands that have the same five cards but are given in different orders (e.g. the 2, 3, 4, 5, 6 of spades and the 6, 5, 4, 3, 2 of spades) are considered the same hand. Therefore, the order of the five cards does not matter. Since there are only 13 spades in a standard deck, calculate the number of combinations of five cards that can be formed from the 13 spades. This value is given by $\binom{13}{5}$:

$$\begin{aligned}
\binom{13}{5} &= \frac{13!}{5!(13-5)!} \\
\\
&= \frac{13 \times 12 \times ... \times 1}{(5 \times 4 \times ... \times 1) \times (8 \times 7 \times ... \times 1)} \\
\\
&= \frac{13 \times 12 \times 11 \times 10 \times 9}{5 \times 4 \times 3 \times 2 \times 1} \\
\\
&= \frac{154,440}{120} \\
\\
&= 1287
\end{aligned}$$

Thus, there are 1287 different five-card hands that consist only of spades.

Functions and Trigonometry

1. C: Calculate $f\left(-\frac{1}{2}\right)$ by substituting $-\frac{1}{2}$ for x in $4x^3 + 5x^2 - 2$ and simplifying the result:

$$f\left(-\tfrac{1}{2}\right) = 4\left(-\tfrac{1}{2}\right)^3 + 5\left(-\tfrac{1}{2}\right)^2 - 2$$

$$= 4\left(-\tfrac{1}{8}\right) + 5\left(\tfrac{1}{4}\right) - 2$$

$$= -\tfrac{1}{2} + \tfrac{5}{4} - 2$$

$$= -\tfrac{5}{4}$$

2. A: The domain of a function is the set of all possible input values that can be evaluated by a function. The easiest way to find the domain of the given function g is to look at all the different operations that are used in the function to determine if one or more of them is not defined for some values of x. The domain will be the set of all real numbers, except those x-values.

Since $g(x)$ is a rational function with $x + 2$ in the denominator and division by zero is undefined, the domain of the function is all real numbers except $x = -2$, which is usually written as $x \neq -2$.

3. B: The composition of two functions is a function that is formed by combining the two functions so that the output of one of them is the input of the other. Find the composition by substituting the output of $g(x)$, $\frac{3x+1}{2}$, for the input of $f(x)$, x, and simplifying the result:

$$(f \circ g)(x) = f\left(\tfrac{3x+1}{2}\right)$$

$$= 2\left(\tfrac{3x+1}{2}\right) - 4$$
$$= (3x + 1) - 4$$

$$= 3x - 3$$

4. C: The inverse of a function is a function that undoes the original function. To find $h^{-1}(x)$, start with the definition of $h(x)$ and then replace $h(x)$ with y:

$$h(x) = \log_{10}(x + 2)$$

$$y = \log_{10}(x + 2)$$

Then switch all of the x's and y's:

$$x = \log_{10}(y + 2)$$

Next solve the resulting equation for y. The logarithm of a number is the exponent that the base must to be raised to in order to get that number. Using this definition, rewrite the logarithmic equation as an exponential one and then solve for y:

$$y + 2 = 10^x$$

$$y = 10^x - 2$$

Finally, replace y with $h^{-1}(x)$:

$$h^{-1}(x) = 10^x - 2$$

5. D: Trigonometric functions are functions of an angle that are based on the proportions of a right triangle. Given that $\sin \theta = \frac{5}{7}$, and $sin = \frac{opposite}{hypotenuse}$, the side opposite θ is 5 units long and the hypotenuse is 7 units long. The remaining side length is an unknown, x.

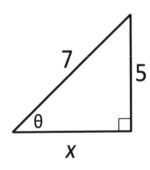

Calculate the missing side x using the Pythagorean Theorem:

$$a^2 + b^2 = c^2$$

$$x^2 + 5^2 = 7^2$$

$$x^2 + 25 = 49$$

$$x^2 = 24$$

$$x = 2\sqrt{6}$$

Finally, calculate the value of cos θ:

$$\cos\theta = \frac{\text{adjacent}}{\text{hypotenuse}}$$

$$= \frac{2\sqrt{6}}{7}$$

Secret Key #1 - Time is Your Greatest Enemy

Pace Yourself

Wear a watch. At the beginning of the test, check the time (or start a chronometer on your watch to count the minutes), and check the time after every few questions to make sure you are "on schedule."

If you are forced to speed up, do it efficiently. Usually one or more answer choices can be eliminated without too much difficulty. Above all, don't panic. Don't speed up and just begin guessing at random choices. By pacing yourself, and continually monitoring your progress against your watch, you will always know exactly how far ahead or behind you are with your available time. If you find that you are one minute behind on the test, don't skip one question without spending any time on it, just to catch back up. Take 15 fewer seconds on the next four questions, and after four questions you'll have caught back up. Once you catch back up, you can continue working each problem at your normal pace.

Furthermore, don't dwell on the problems that you were rushed on. If a problem was taking up too much time and you made a hurried guess, it must be difficult. The difficult questions are the ones you are most likely to miss anyway, so it isn't a big loss. It is better to end with more time than you need than to run out of time.

Lastly, sometimes it is beneficial to slow down if you are constantly getting ahead of time. You are always more likely to catch a careless mistake by working more slowly than quickly, and among very high-scoring test takers (those who are likely to have lots of time left over), careless errors affect the score more than mastery of material.

Secret Key #2 - Guessing is not Guesswork

You probably know that guessing is a good idea. Unlike other standardized tests, there is no penalty for getting a wrong answer. Even if you have no idea about a question, you still have a 20-25% chance of getting it right.

Most test takers do not understand the impact that proper guessing can have on their score. Unless you score extremely high, guessing will significantly contribute to your final score.

Monkeys Take the Test

What most test takers don't realize is that to insure that 20-25% chance, you have to guess randomly. If you put 20 monkeys in a room to take this test, assuming they answered once per question and behaved themselves, on average they would get 20-25% of the questions correct. Put 20 test takers in the room, and the average will be much lower among guessed questions. Why?
1. The test writers intentionally write deceptive answer choices that "look" right. A test taker has no idea about a question, so he picks the "best looking" answer, which is often wrong. The monkey has no idea what looks good and what doesn't, so it will consistently be right about 20-25% of the time.
2. Test takers will eliminate answer choices from the guessing pool based on a hunch or intuition. Simple but correct answers often get excluded, leaving a 0% chance of being correct. The monkey has no clue, and often gets lucky with the best choice.

This is why the process of elimination endorsed by most test courses is flawed and detrimental to your performance. Test takers don't guess; they make an ignorant stab in the dark that is usually worse than random.

$5 Challenge

Let me introduce one of the most valuable ideas of this course—the $5 challenge:

You only mark your "best guess" if you are willing to bet $5 on it.
You only eliminate choices from guessing if you are willing to bet $5 on it.

Why $5? Five dollars is an amount of money that is small yet not insignificant, and can really add up fast (20 questions could cost you $100). Likewise, each answer choice on one question of the test will have a small impact on your overall score, but it can really add up to a lot of points in the end.

The process of elimination IS valuable. The following shows your chance of guessing it right:

If you eliminate wrong answer choices until only this many remain:	Chance of getting it correct:
1	100%
2	50%
3	33%

However, if you accidentally eliminate the right answer or go on a hunch for an incorrect answer, your chances drop dramatically—to 0%. By guessing among all the answer choices, you are GUARANTEED to have a shot at the right answer.

That's why the $5 test is so valuable. If you give up the advantage and safety of a pure guess, it had better be worth the risk.

What we still haven't covered is how to be sure that whatever guess you make is truly random. Here's the easiest way:

Always pick the first answer choice among those remaining.

Such a technique means that you have decided, **before you see a single test question**, exactly how you are going to guess, and since the order of choices tells you nothing about which one is correct, this guessing technique is perfectly random. This section is not meant to scare you away from making educated guesses or eliminating choices; you just need to define when a choice is worth eliminating. The $5 test, along with a pre-defined random guessing strategy, is the best way to make sure you reap all of the benefits of guessing.

Secret Key #3 - Practice Smarter, Not Harder

Many test takers delay the test preparation process because they dread the awful amounts of practice time they think necessary to succeed on the test. We have refined an effective method that will take you only a fraction of the time.

There are a number of "obstacles" in the path to success. Among these are answering questions, finishing in time, and mastering test-taking strategies. All must be executed on the day of the test at peak performance, or your score will suffer. The test is a mental marathon that has a large impact on your future.

Just like a marathon runner, it is important to work your way up to the full challenge. So first you just worry about questions, and then time, and finally strategy:

Success Strategy

1. Find a good source for practice tests.
2. If you are willing to make a larger time investment, consider using more than one study guide. Often the different approaches of multiple authors will help you "get" difficult concepts.
3. Take a practice test with no time constraints, with all study helps, "open book." Take your time with questions and focus on applying strategies.
4. Take a practice test with time constraints, with all guides, "open book."
5. Take a final practice test without open material and with time limits.

If you have time to take more practice tests, just repeat step 5. By gradually exposing yourself to the full rigors of the test environment, you will condition your mind to the stress of test day and maximize your success.

Secret Key #4 - Prepare, Don't Procrastinate

Let me state an obvious fact: if you take the test three times, you will probably get three different scores. This is due to the way you feel on test day, the level of preparedness you have, and the version of the test you see. Despite the test writers' claims to the contrary, some versions of the test WILL be easier for you than others. Since your future depends so much on your score, you should maximize your chances of success. In order to maximize the likelihood of success, you've got to prepare in advance. This means taking practice tests and spending time learning the information and test taking strategies you will need to succeed.

Never go take the actual test as a "practice" test, expecting that you can just take it again if you need to. Take all the practice tests you can on your own, but when you go to take the official test, be prepared, be focused, and do your best the first time!

Secret Key #5 - Test Yourself

Everyone knows that time is money. There is no need to spend too much of your time or too little of your time preparing for the test. You should only spend as much of your precious time preparing as is necessary for you to get the score you need.

Once you have taken a practice test under real conditions of time constraints, then you will know if you are ready for the test or not.

If you have scored extremely high the first time that you take the practice test, then there is not much point in spending countless hours studying. You are already there.

Benchmark your abilities by retaking practice tests and seeing how much you have improved. Once you consistently score high enough to guarantee success, then you are ready.

If you have scored well below where you need, then knuckle down and begin studying in earnest. Check your improvement regularly through the use of practice tests under real conditions. Above all, don't worry, panic, or give up. The key is perseverance!

Then, when you go to take the test, remain confident and remember how well you did on the practice tests. If you can score high enough on a practice test, then you can do the same on the real thing.

General Strategies

The most important thing you can do is to ignore your fears and jump into the test immediately. Do not be overwhelmed by any strange-sounding terms. You have to jump into the test like jumping into a pool—all at once is the easiest way.

Make Predictions

As you read and understand the question, try to guess what the answer will be. Remember that several of the answer choices are wrong, and once you begin reading them, your mind will immediately become cluttered with answer choices designed to throw you off. Your mind is typically the most focused immediately after you have read the question and digested its contents. If you can, try to predict what the correct answer will be. You may be surprised at what you can predict. Quickly scan the choices and see if your prediction is in the listed answer choices. If it is, then you can be quite confident that you have the right answer. It still won't hurt to check the other answer choices, but most of the time, you've got it!

Answer the Question

It may seem obvious to only pick answer choices that answer the question, but the test writers can create some excellent answer choices that are wrong. Don't pick an answer just because it sounds right, or you believe it to be true. It MUST answer the question. Once you've made your selection, always go back and check it against the question and make sure that you didn't misread the question and that the answer choice does answer the question posed.

Benchmark

After you read the first answer choice, decide if you think it sounds correct or not. If it doesn't, move on to the next answer choice. If it does, mentally mark that answer choice. This doesn't mean that you've definitely selected it as your answer choice, it just means that it's the best you've seen thus far. Go ahead and read the next choice. If the next choice is worse than the one you've already selected, keep going to the next answer choice. If the next choice is better than the choice you've already selected, mentally mark the new answer choice as your best guess.

The first answer choice that you select becomes your standard. Every other answer choice must be benchmarked against that standard. That choice is correct until proven otherwise by another answer choice beating it out. Once you've decided that no other answer choice seems as good, do one final check to ensure that your answer choice answers the question posed.

Valid Information

Don't discount any of the information provided in the question. Every piece of information may be necessary to determine the correct answer. None of the information in the question is there to throw you off (while the answer choices will certainly have information to throw you off). If two seemingly unrelated topics are discussed, don't ignore either. You can be confident there is a relationship, or it wouldn't be included in the question, and you are probably going to have to determine what is that relationship to find the answer.

Avoid "Fact Traps"

Don't get distracted by a choice that is factually true. Your search is for the answer that answers the question. Stay focused and don't fall for an answer that is true but irrelevant. Always go back to the question and make sure you're choosing an answer that actually answers the question and is not just a true statement. An answer can be factually correct, but it MUST answer the question asked. Additionally, two answers can both be seemingly correct, so be sure to read all of the answer choices, and make sure that you get the one that BEST answers the question.

Milk the Question

Some of the questions may throw you completely off. They might deal with a subject you have not been exposed to, or one that you haven't reviewed in years. While your lack of knowledge about the subject will be a hindrance, the question itself can give you many clues that will help you find the correct answer. Read the question carefully and look for clues. Watch particularly for adjectives and nouns describing difficult terms or words that you don't recognize. Regardless of whether you completely understand a word or not, replacing it with a synonym, either provided or one you more familiar with, may help you to understand what the questions are asking. Rather than wracking your mind about specific detailed information concerning a difficult term or word, try to use mental substitutes that are easier to understand.

The Trap of Familiarity

Don't just choose a word because you recognize it. On difficult questions, you may not recognize a number of words in the answer choices. The test writers don't put "make-believe" words on the test, so don't think that just because you only recognize all the words in one answer choice that that answer choice must be correct. If you only recognize words in one answer choice, then focus on that one. Is it correct? Try your best to determine if it is correct. If it is, that's great. If not, eliminate it. Each word and answer choice you eliminate increases your chances of getting the question correct, even if you then have to guess among the unfamiliar choices.

Eliminate Answers

Eliminate choices as soon as you realize they are wrong. But be careful! Make sure you consider all of the possible answer choices. Just because one appears right, doesn't mean that the next one won't be even better! The test writers will usually put more than one good answer choice for every question, so read all of them. Don't worry if you are stuck between two that seem right. By getting down to just two remaining possible choices, your odds are now 50/50. Rather than wasting too much time, play the odds. You are guessing, but guessing wisely because you've been able to knock out some of the answer choices that you know are wrong. If you are eliminating choices and realize that the last answer choice you are left with is also obviously wrong, don't panic. Start over and consider each choice again. There may easily be something that you missed the first time and will realize on the second pass.

Tough Questions

If you are stumped on a problem or it appears too hard or too difficult, don't waste time. Move on! Remember though, if you can quickly check for obviously incorrect answer choices, your chances of guessing correctly are greatly improved. Before you completely give up, at least try to knock out a couple of possible answers. Eliminate what you can and then guess at the remaining answer choices before moving on.

Brainstorm

If you get stuck on a difficult question, spend a few seconds quickly brainstorming. Run through the complete list of possible answer choices. Look at each choice and ask yourself, "Could this answer the question satisfactorily?" Go through each answer choice and consider it independently of the others. By systematically going through all possibilities, you may find something that you would otherwise overlook. Remember though that when you get stuck, it's important to try to keep moving.

Read Carefully

Understand the problem. Read the question and answer choices carefully. Don't miss the question because you misread the terms. You have plenty of time to read each question thoroughly and make sure you understand what is being asked. Yet a happy medium must be attained, so don't waste too much time. You must read carefully, but efficiently.

Face Value

When in doubt, use common sense. Always accept the situation in the problem at face value. Don't read too much into it. These problems will not require you to make huge leaps of logic. The test writers aren't trying to throw you off with a cheap trick. If you have to go beyond creativity and make a leap of logic in order to have an answer choice answer the question, then you should look at the other answer choices. Don't overcomplicate the problem by creating theoretical relationships or explanations that will warp time or space. These are normal problems rooted in reality. It's just that the applicable relationship or explanation may not be readily apparent and you have to figure things out. Use your common sense to interpret anything that isn't clear.

Prefixes

If you're having trouble with a word in the question or answer choices, try dissecting it. Take advantage of every clue that the word might include. Prefixes and suffixes can be a huge help. Usually they allow you to determine a basic meaning. Pre- means before, post- means after, pro - is positive, de- is negative. From these prefixes and suffixes, you can get an idea of the general meaning of the word and try to put it into context. Beware though of any traps. Just because con- is the opposite of pro-, doesn't necessarily mean congress is the opposite of progress!

Hedge Phrases

Watch out for critical hedge phrases, led off with words such as "likely," "may," "can," "sometimes," "often," "almost," "mostly," "usually," "generally," "rarely," and "sometimes." Question writers insert these hedge phrases to cover every possibility. Often an answer choice will be wrong simply because it leaves no room for exception. Unless the situation calls for them, avoid answer choices that have definitive words like "exactly," and "always."

Switchback Words

Stay alert for "switchbacks." These are the words and phrases frequently used to alert you to shifts in thought. The most common switchback word is "but." Others include "although," "however," "nevertheless," "on the other hand," "even though," "while," "in spite of," "despite," and "regardless of."

New Information

Correct answer choices will rarely have completely new information included. Answer choices typically are straightforward reflections of the material asked about and will directly relate to the question. If a new piece of information is included in an answer choice that doesn't even seem to relate to the topic being asked about, then that answer choice is likely incorrect. All of the information needed to answer the question is usually provided for you in the question. You should not have to make guesses that are unsupported or choose answer choices that require unknown information that cannot be reasoned from what is given.

Time Management

On technical questions, don't get lost on the technical terms. Don't spend too much time on any one question. If you don't know what a term means, then odds are you aren't going to get much further since you don't have a dictionary. You should be able to immediately recognize whether or not you know a term. If you don't, work with the other clues that you have—the other answer choices and terms provided— but don't waste too much time trying to figure out a difficult term that you don't know.

Contextual Clues

Look for contextual clues. An answer can be right but not the correct answer. The contextual clues will help you find the answer that is most right and is correct. Understand the context in which a phrase or statement is made. This will help you make important distinctions.

Don't Panic

Panicking will not answer any questions for you; therefore, it isn't helpful. When you first see the question, if your mind goes blank, take a deep breath. Force yourself to mechanically go through the steps of solving the problem using the strategies you've learned.

Pace Yourself

Don't get clock fever. It's easy to be overwhelmed when you're looking at a page full of questions, your mind is full of random thoughts and feeling confused, and the clock is ticking down faster than you would like. Calm down and maintain the pace that you have set for yourself. As long as you are on track by monitoring your pace, you are guaranteed to have enough time for yourself. When you get to the last few minutes of the test, it may seem like you won't have enough time left, but if you only have as many questions as you should have left at that point, then you're right on track!

Answer Selection

The best way to pick an answer choice is to eliminate all of those that are wrong, until only one is left and confirm that is the correct answer. Sometimes though, an answer choice may immediately look right. Be careful! Take a second to make sure that the other choices are not equally obvious. Don't make a hasty mistake. There are only two times that you should stop before checking other answers. First is when you are positive that the answer choice you have selected is correct. Second is when time is almost out and you have to make a quick guess!

Check Your Work

Since you will probably not know every term listed and the answer to every question, it is important that you get credit for the ones that you do know. Don't miss any questions through careless mistakes. If at all possible, try to take a second to look back over your answer selection and make sure you've selected the correct answer choice and haven't made a costly careless mistake (such as marking an answer choice that you didn't mean to mark). The time it takes for this quick double check should more than pay for itself in caught mistakes.

Beware of Directly Quoted Answers

Sometimes an answer choice will repeat word for word a portion of the question or reference section. However, beware of such exact duplication. It may be a trap! More than likely, the correct choice will paraphrase or summarize a point, rather than being exactly the same wording.

Slang

Scientific sounding answers are better than slang ones. An answer choice that begins "To compare the outcomes..." is much more likely to be correct than one that begins "Because some people insisted..."

Extreme Statements

Avoid wild answers that throw out highly controversial ideas that are proclaimed as established fact. An answer choice that states the "process should used in certain situations, if…" is much more likely to be correct than one that states the "process should be discontinued completely." The first is a calm rational statement and doesn't even make a definitive, uncompromising stance, using a hedge word "if" to provide wiggle room, whereas the second choice is a radical idea and far more extreme.

Answer Choice Families

When you have two or more answer choices that are direct opposites or parallels, one of them is usually the correct answer. For instance, if one answer choice states "x increases" and another answer choice states "x decreases" or "y increases," then those two or three answer choices are very similar in construction and fall into the same family of answer choices. A family of answer choices consists of two or three answer choices, very similar in construction, but often with directly opposite meanings. Usually the correct answer choice will be in that family of answer choices. The "odd man out" or answer choice that doesn't seem to fit the parallel construction of the other answer choices is more likely to be incorrect.

How to Overcome Your Fear of Math

The word *math* is enough to strike fear into most hearts. How many of us have memories of sitting through confusing lectures, wrestling over mind-numbing homework, or taking tests that still seem incomprehensible even after hours of study? Years after graduation, many still shudder at these memories.

The fact is, math is not just a classroom subject. It has real-world implications that you face every day, whether you realize it or not. This may be balancing your monthly budget, deciding how many supplies to buy for a project, or simply splitting a meal check with friends. The idea of daily confrontations with math can be so paralyzing that some develop a condition known as *math anxiety*.

But you do NOT need to be paralyzed by this anxiety! In fact, while you may have thought all your life that you're not good at math, or that your brain isn't wired to understand it, the truth is that you may have been conditioned to think this way. From your earliest school days, the way you were taught affected the way you viewed different subjects. And the way math has been taught has changed.

Several decades ago, there was a shift in American math classrooms. The focus changed from traditional problem-solving to a conceptual view of topics, de-emphasizing the importance of learning the basics and building on them. The solid foundation necessary for math progression and confidence was undermined. Math became more of a vague concept than a concrete idea. Today, it is common to think of math, not as a straightforward system, but as a mysterious, complicated method that can't be fully understood unless you're a genius.

This is why you may still have nightmares about being called on to answer a difficult problem in front of the class. Math anxiety is a very real, though unnecessary, fear.

Math anxiety may begin with a single class period. Let's say you missed a day in 6th grade math and never quite understood the concept that was taught while you were gone. Since math is cumulative, with each new concept building on past ones, this could very well affect the rest of your math career. Without that one day's knowledge, it will be difficult to understand any other concepts that link to it. Rather than realizing that you're just missing one key piece, you may begin to believe that you're simply not capable of understanding math.

This belief can change the way you approach other classes, career options, and everyday life experiences, if you become anxious at the thought that math might be required. A student who loves science may choose a different path of study upon realizing that multiple math classes will be required for a degree. An aspiring medical student may hesitate at the thought of going through the necessary math classes. For some this anxiety escalates into a more extreme state known as *math phobia*.

Math anxiety is challenging to address because it is rooted deeply and may come from a variety of causes: an embarrassing moment in class, a teacher who did not explain concepts well and contributed to a shaky foundation, or a failed test that contributed to the belief of math failure.

These causes add up over time, encouraged by society's popular view that math is hard and unpleasant. Eventually a person comes to firmly believe that he or she is simply bad at math. This belief makes it difficult to grasp new concepts or even remember old ones. Homework and test grades begin to slip, which only confirms the belief. The poor performance is not due to lack of ability but is caused by math anxiety.

Math anxiety is an emotional issue, not a lack of intelligence. But when it becomes deeply rooted, it can become more than just an emotional problem. Physical symptoms appear. Blood pressure may rise and heartbeat may quicken at the sight of a math problem – or even the thought of math! This fear leads to a mental block. When someone with math anxiety is asked to perform a calculation, even a basic problem can seem overwhelming and impossible. The emotional and physical response to the thought of math prevents the brain from working through it logically.

The more this happens, the more a person's confidence drops, and the more math anxiety is generated. This vicious cycle must be broken!

The first step in breaking the cycle is to go back to very beginning and make sure you really understand the basics of how math works and why it works. It is not enough to memorize rules for multiplication and division. If you don't know WHY these rules work, your foundation will be shaky and you will be at risk of developing a phobia. Understanding mathematical concepts not only promotes confidence and security, but allows you to build on this understanding for new concepts. Additionally, you can solve unfamiliar problems using familiar concepts and processes.

Why is it that students in other countries regularly outperform American students in math? The answer likely boils down to a couple of things: the foundation of mathematical conceptual understanding and societal perception. While students in the US are not expected to *like* or *get* math, in many other nations, students are expected not only to understand math but also to excel at it.

Changing the American view of math that leads to math anxiety is a monumental task. It requires changing the training of teachers nationwide, from kindergarten through high school, so that they learn to teach the *why* behind math and to combat the wrong math views that students may develop. It also involves changing the stigma associated with math, so that it is no longer viewed as unpleasant and incomprehensible. While these are necessary changes, they are challenging and will take time. But in the meantime, math anxiety is not irreversible – it can be faced and defeated, one person at a time.

False Beliefs

One reason math anxiety has taken such hold is that several false beliefs have been created and shared until they became widely accepted. Some of these unhelpful beliefs include the following:

- *There is only one way to solve a math problem.* In the same way that you can choose from different driving routes and still arrive at the same house, you can solve a math problem using different methods and still find the correct answer. A person who understands the reasoning behind math calculations may be able to look at an unfamiliar concept and find the right answer, just by applying logic to the knowledge they already have. This approach may be different than what is taught in the classroom, but it is still valid. Unfortunately, even many teachers view math as a subject where the best course of action is to memorize the rule or process for each problem rather than as a place for students to exercise logic and creativity in finding a solution.
- *Many people don't have a mind for math.* A person who has struggled due to poor teaching or math anxiety may falsely believe that he or she doesn't have the mental capacity to grasp mathematical concepts. Most of the time, this is false. Many people find that when they are relieved of their math anxiety, they have more than enough brainpower to understand math.
- *Men are naturally better at math than women.* Even though research has shown this to be false, many young women still avoid math careers and classes because of their belief that their math abilities are inferior. Many girls have come to believe that math is a male skill and have given up trying to understand or enjoy it.
- *Counting aids are bad.* Something like counting on your fingers or drawing out a problem to visualize it may be frowned on as childish or a crutch, but these devices can help you get a tangible understanding of a problem or a concept.

Sadly, many students buy into these ideologies at an early age. A young girl who enjoys math class may be conditioned to think that she doesn't actually have the brain for it because math is for boys, and may turn her energies to other pursuits, permanently closing the door on a wide range of opportunities. A child who finds the right answer but doesn't follow the teacher's method may believe that he is doing it wrong and isn't good at math. A student who never had a problem with math before may have a poor teacher and become confused, yet believe that the problem is because she doesn't have a mathematical mind.

Students who have bought into these erroneous beliefs quickly begin to add their own anxieties, adapting them to their own personal situations:

- *I'll never use this in real life.* A huge number of people wrongly believe that math is irrelevant outside the classroom. By adopting this mindset, they are handicapping themselves for a life in a mathematical world, as well as limiting their career choices. When they are inevitably faced with real-world math, they are conditioning themselves to respond with anxiety.
- *I'm not quick enough.* While timed tests and quizzes, or even simply comparing yourself with other students in the class, can lead to this belief, speed is not an indicator of skill level. A person can work very slowly yet understand at a deep level.
- *If I can understand it, it's too easy.* People with a low view of their own abilities tend to think that if they are able to grasp a concept, it must be simple. They cannot accept the idea that they are capable of understanding math. This belief will make it harder to learn, no matter how intelligent they are.
- *I just can't learn this.* An overwhelming number of people think this, from young children to adults, and much of the time it is simply not true. But this mindset can turn into a self-fulfilling prophecy that keeps you from exercising and growing your math ability.

The good news is, each of these myths can be debunked. For most people, they are based on emotion and psychology, NOT on actual ability! It will take time, effort, and the desire to change, but change is possible. Even if you have spent years thinking that you don't have the capability to understand math, it is not too late to uncover your true ability and find relief from the anxiety that surrounds math.

Math Strategies

It is important to have a plan of attack to combat math anxiety. There are many useful strategies for pinpointing the fears or myths and eradicating them:

Go back to the basics. For most people, math anxiety stems from a poor foundation. You may think that you have a complete understanding of addition and subtraction, or even decimals and percentages, but make absolutely sure. Learning math is different from learning other subjects. For example, when you learn history, you study various time periods and places and events. It may be important to memorize dates or find out about the lives of famous people. When you move from US history to world history, there will be some overlap, but a large amount of the information will be new. Mathematical concepts, on the other hand, are very closely linked and highly dependent on each other. It's like climbing a ladder – if a rung is missing from your understanding, it may be difficult or impossible for you to climb any higher, no matter how hard you try. So go back and make sure your math foundation is strong. This may mean taking a remedial math course, going to a tutor to work through the shaky concepts, or just going through your old homework to make sure you really understand it.

Speak the language. Math has a large vocabulary of terms and phrases unique to working problems. Sometimes these are completely new terms, and sometimes they are common words, but are used differently in a math setting. If you can't speak the language, it will be very difficult to get a thorough understanding of the concepts. It's common for students to think that they don't understand math when they simply don't understand the vocabulary. The good news is that this is fairly easy to fix. Brushing up on any terms you aren't quite sure of can help bring the rest of the concepts into focus.

Check your anxiety level. When you think about math, do you feel nervous or uncomfortable? Do you struggle with feelings of inadequacy, even on concepts that you know you've already learned? It's important to understand your specific math anxieties, and what triggers them. When you catch yourself falling back on a false belief, mentally replace it with the truth. Don't let yourself believe that you can't learn, or that struggling with a concept means you'll never understand it. Instead, remind yourself of how much you've already learned and dwell on that past success. Visualize grasping the new concept, linking it to your old knowledge, and moving on to the next challenge. Also, learn how to manage anxiety when it arises. There are many techniques for coping with the irrational fears that rise to the surface when you enter the math classroom. This may include controlled breathing, replacing negative thoughts with positive ones, or visualizing success. Anxiety interferes with your ability to concentrate and absorb information, which in turn contributes to greater anxiety. If you can learn how to regain control of your thinking, you will be better able to pay attention, make progress, and succeed!

Don't go it alone. Like any deeply ingrained belief, math anxiety is not easy to eradicate. And there is no need for you to wrestle through it on your own. It will take time, and many people find that speaking with a counselor or psychiatrist helps. They can help you develop strategies for responding to anxiety and overcoming old ideas. Additionally, it can be very helpful to take a short course or seek out a math tutor to help you find and fix the missing rungs on your ladder and make sure that you're ready to progress to the next level. You can also find a number of math aids online: courses that will teach you mental devices for figuring out problems, how to get the most out of your math classes, etc.

Check your math attitude. No matter how much you want to learn and overcome your anxiety, you'll have trouble if you still have a negative attitude toward math. If you think it's too hard, or just have general feelings of dread about math, it will be hard to learn and to break through the anxiety. Work on cultivating a positive math attitude. Remind yourself that math is not just a hurdle to be cleared, but a valuable asset. When you view math with a positive attitude, you'll be much more likely to understand and even enjoy it. This is something you must do for yourself. You may find it helpful to visit with a counselor. Your tutor, friends, and family may cheer you on in your endeavors. But your greatest asset is yourself. You are inside your own mind – tell yourself what you need to hear. Relive past victories. Remind yourself that you are capable of understanding math. Root out any false beliefs that linger and replace them with positive truths. Even if it doesn't feel true at first, it will begin to affect your thinking and pave the way for a positive, anxiety-free mindset.

Aside from these general strategies, there are a number of specific practical things you can do to begin your journey toward overcoming math anxiety. Something as simple as learning a new note-taking strategy can change the way you approach math and give you more confidence and understanding. New study techniques can also make a huge difference.

Math anxiety leads to bad habits. If it causes you to be afraid of answering a question in class, you may gravitate toward the back row. You may be embarrassed to ask for help. And you may procrastinate on assignments, which leads to rushing through them at the last moment when it's too late to get a better understanding. It's important to identify your negative behaviors and replace them with positive ones:

Prepare ahead of time. Read the lesson before you go to class. Being exposed to the topics that will be covered in class ahead of time, even if you don't understand them perfectly, is extremely helpful in increasing what you retain from the lecture. Do your homework and, if you're still shaky, go over some extra problems. The key to a solid understanding of math is practice.

Sit front and center. When you can easily see and hear, you'll understand more, and you'll avoid the distractions of other students if no one is in front of you. Plus, you're more likely to be sitting with students who are positive and engaged, rather than others with math anxiety. Let their positive math attitude rub off on you.

Ask questions in class and out. If you don't understand something, just ask. If you need a more in-depth explanation, the teacher may need to work with you outside of class, but often it's a simple concept you don't quite understand, and a single question may clear it up. If you wait, you may not be able to follow the rest of the day's lesson. For extra help, most professors have office hours outside of class when you can go over concepts one-on-one to clear up any uncertainties. Additionally, there may be a *math lab* or study session you can attend for homework help. Take advantage of this.

Review. Even if you feel that you've fully mastered a concept, review it periodically to reinforce it. Going over an old lesson has several benefits: solidifying your

Copyright © Mometrix Media. You have been licensed one copy of this document for personal use only. Any other reproduction or redistribution is strictly prohibited. All rights reserved.

understanding, giving you a confidence boost, and even giving some new insights into material that you're currently learning! Don't let yourself get rusty. That can lead to problems with learning later concepts.

Teaching Tips

While the math student's mindset is the most crucial to overcoming math anxiety, it is also important for others to adjust their math attitudes. Teachers and parents have an enormous influence on how students relate to math. They can either contribute to math confidence or math anxiety.

As a parent or teacher, it is very important to convey a positive math attitude. Retelling horror stories of your own bad experience with math will contribute to a new generation of math anxiety. Even if you don't share your experiences, others will be able to sense your fears and may begin to believe them.

Even a careless comment can have a big impact, so watch for phrases like "He's not good at math" or "I never liked math." You are a crucial role model, and your children or students will unconsciously adopt your mindset. Give them a positive example to follow. Rather than teaching them to fear the math world before they even know it, teach them about all its potential and excitement.

Work to present math as an integral, beautiful, and understandable part of life. Encourage creativity in solving problems. Watch for false beliefs and dispel them. Cross the lines between subjects: integrate history, English, and music with math. Show students how math is used every day, and how the entire world is based on mathematical principles, from the pull of gravity to the shape of seashells. Instead of letting students see math as a necessary evil, direct them to view it as an imaginative, beautiful art form – an art form that they are capable of mastering and using.

Don't give too narrow a view of math. It is more than just numbers. Yes, working problems and learning formulas is a large part of classroom math. But don't let the teaching stop there. Teach students about the everyday implications of math. Show them how nature works according to the laws of mathematics, and take them outside to make discoveries of their own. Expose them to math-related careers by inviting visiting speakers, asking students to do research and presentations, and learning students' interests and aptitudes on a personal level.

Demonstrate the importance of math. Many people see math as nothing more than a required stepping stone to their degree, a nuisance with no real usefulness. Teach students that algebra is used every day in managing their bank accounts, in following recipes, and in scheduling the day's events. Show them how learning to do geometric proofs helps them to develop logical thinking, an invaluable life skill. Let them see that math surrounds them and is integrally linked to their daily lives: that weather predictions are based on math, that math was used to design cars and other machines, etc. Most of all, give them the tools to use math to enrich their lives.

Make math as tangible as possible. Use visual aids and objects that can be touched. It is much easier to grasp a concept when you can hold it in your hands and manipulate it, rather than just listening to the lecture. Encourage math outside of the classroom. The real world is full of measuring, counting, and calculating, so let students participate in this. Keep your eyes open for numbers and patterns to discuss. Talk about how scores are calculated in sports games and how far apart plants are placed in a garden row for maximum growth. Build the mindset that math is a normal and interesting part of daily life.

Finally, find math resources that help to build a positive math attitude. There are a number of books that show math as fascinating and exciting while teaching important concepts, for example: *The Math Curse; A Wrinkle in Time; The Phantom Tollbooth;* and *Fractals, Googols and Other Mathematical Tales.* You can also find a number of online resources: math puzzles and games, videos that show math in nature, and communities of math enthusiasts. On a local level, students can compete in a variety of math competitions with other schools or join a math club.

The student who experiences math as exciting and interesting is unlikely to suffer from math anxiety. Going through life without this handicap is an immense advantage and opens many doors that others have closed through their fear.

Self-Check

Whether you suffer from math anxiety or not, chances are that you have been exposed to some of the false beliefs mentioned above. Now is the time to check yourself for any errors you may have accepted. Do you think you're not wired for math? Or that you don't need to understand it since you're not planning on a math career? Do you think math is just too difficult for the average person?

Find the errors you've taken to heart and replace them with positive thinking. Are you capable of learning math? Yes! Can you control your anxiety? Yes! These errors will resurface from time to time, so be watchful. Don't let others with math anxiety influence you or sway your confidence. If you're having trouble with a concept, find help. Don't let it discourage you!

Create a plan of attack for defeating math anxiety and sharpening your skills. Do some research and decide if it would help you to take a class, get a tutor, or find some online resources to fine-tune your knowledge. Make the effort to get good nutrition, hydration, and sleep so that you are operating at full capacity. Remind yourself daily that you are skilled and that anxiety does not control you. Your mind is capable of so much more than you know. Give it the tools it needs to grow and thrive.

Special Report: How to Overcome Test Anxiety

The very nature of tests caters to some level of anxiety, nervousness, or tension, just as we feel for any important event that occurs in our lives. A little bit of anxiety or nervousness can be a good thing. It helps us with motivation, and makes achievement just that much sweeter. However, too much anxiety can be a problem, especially if it hinders our ability to function and perform.

"Test anxiety," is the term that refers to the emotional reactions that some test-takers experience when faced with a test or exam. Having a fear of testing and exams is based upon a rational fear, since the test-taker's performance can shape the course of an academic career. Nevertheless, experiencing excessive fear of examinations will only interfere with the test-taker's ability to perform and chance to be successful.

There are a large variety of causes that can contribute to the development and sensation of test anxiety. These include, but are not limited to, lack of preparation and worrying about issues surrounding the test.

Lack of Preparation

Lack of preparation can be identified by the following behaviors or situations:

Not scheduling enough time to study, and therefore cramming the night before the test or exam
Managing time poorly, to create the sensation that there is not enough time to do everything
Failing to organize the text information in advance, so that the study material consists of the entire text and not simply the pertinent information
Poor overall studying habits

Worrying, on the other hand, can be related to both the test taker, or many other factors around him/her that will be affected by the results of the test. These include worrying about:

Previous performances on similar exams, or exams in general
How friends and other students are achieving
The negative consequences that will result from a poor grade or failure

There are three primary elements to test anxiety. Physical components, which involve the same typical bodily reactions as those to acute anxiety (to be discussed below). Emotional factors have to do with fear or panic. Mental or cognitive issues concerning attention spans and memory abilities.

Physical Signals

There are many different symptoms of test anxiety, and these are not limited to mental and emotional strain. Frequently there are a range of physical signals that will let a test taker know that he/she is suffering from test anxiety. These bodily changes can include the following:

Perspiring
Sweaty palms
Wet, trembling hands
Nausea
Dry mouth
A knot in the stomach
Headache
Faintness
Muscle tension
Aching shoulders, back and neck
Rapid heart beat
Feeling too hot/cold

To recognize the sensation of test anxiety, a test-taker should monitor him/herself for the following sensations:

The physical distress symptoms as listed above
Emotional sensitivity, expressing emotional feelings such as the need to cry or laugh too much, or a sensation of anger or helplessness
A decreased ability to think, causing the test-taker to blank out or have racing thoughts that are hard to organize or control.

Though most students will feel some level of anxiety when faced with a test or exam, the majority can cope with that anxiety and maintain it at a manageable level. However, those who cannot are faced with a very real and very serious condition, which can and should be controlled for the immeasurable benefit of this sufferer.

Naturally, these sensations lead to negative results for the testing experience. The most common effects of test anxiety have to do with nervousness and mental blocking.

Nervousness

Nervousness can appear in several different levels:

The test-taker's difficulty, or even inability to read and understand the questions on the test
The difficulty or inability to organize thoughts to a coherent form
The difficulty or inability to recall key words and concepts relating to the testing questions (especially essays)
The receipt of poor grades on a test, though the test material was well known by the test taker
Conversely, a person may also experience mental blocking, which involves:

Blanking out on test questions
Only remembering the correct answers to the questions when the test has already finished.

Fortunately for test anxiety sufferers, beating these feelings, to a large degree, has to do with proper preparation. When a test taker has a feeling of preparedness, then anxiety will be dramatically lessened.

The first step to resolving anxiety issues is to distinguish which of the two types of anxiety are being suffered. If the anxiety is a direct result of a lack of preparation, this should be considered a normal reaction, and the anxiety level (as opposed to the test results) shouldn't be anything to worry about. However, if, when adequately prepared, the test-taker still panics, blanks out, or seems to overreact, this is not a fully rational reaction. While this can be considered normal too, there are many ways to combat and overcome these effects.

Remember that anxiety cannot be entirely eliminated, however, there are ways to minimize it, to make the anxiety easier to manage. Preparation is one of the best ways to minimize test anxiety. Therefore the following techniques are wise in order to best fight off any anxiety that may want to build.

To begin with, try to avoid cramming before a test, whenever it is possible. By trying to memorize an entire term's worth of information in one day, you'll be shocking your system, and not giving yourself a very good chance to absorb the information. This is an easy path to anxiety, so for those who suffer from test anxiety, cramming should not even be considered an option.

Instead of cramming, work throughout the semester to combine all of the material which is presented throughout the semester, and work on it gradually as the course goes by, making sure to master the main concepts first, leaving minor details for a week or so before the test.

To study for the upcoming exam, be sure to pose questions that may be on the examination, to gauge the ability to answer them by integrating the ideas from your texts, notes and lectures, as well as any supplementary readings.

If it is truly impossible to cover all of the information that was covered in that particular term, concentrate on the most important portions, that can be covered very well. Learn these concepts as best as possible, so that when the test comes, a goal can be made to use these concepts as presentations of your knowledge.

In addition to study habits, changes in attitude are critical to beating a struggle with test anxiety. In fact, an improvement of the perspective over the entire test-taking experience can actually help a test taker to enjoy studying and therefore improve the overall experience. Be certain not to overemphasize the significance of the grade - know that the result of the test is neither a reflection of self worth, nor is it a measure of intelligence; one grade will not predict a person's future success.

To improve an overall testing outlook, the following steps should be tried:

Keeping in mind that the most reasonable expectation for taking a test is to expect to try to demonstrate as much of what you know as you possibly can. Reminding ourselves that a test is only one test; this is not the only one, and there will be others.
The thought of thinking of oneself in an irrational, all-or-nothing term should be avoided at all costs.
A reward should be designated for after the test, so there's something to look forward to. Whether it be going to a movie, going out to eat, or simply visiting friends, schedule it in advance, and do it no matter what result is expected on the exam.

Test-takers should also keep in mind that the basics are some of the most important things, even beyond anti-anxiety techniques and studying. Never neglect the basic social, emotional and biological needs, in order to try to absorb information. In order to best achieve, these three factors must be held as just as important as the studying itself.

Study Steps

Remember the following important steps for studying:

Maintain healthy nutrition and exercise habits. Continue both your recreational activities and social pass times. These both contribute to your physical and emotional well being.

Be certain to get a good amount of sleep, especially the night before the test, because when you're overtired you are not able to perform to the best of your best ability.

Keep the studying pace to a moderate level by taking breaks when they are needed, and varying the work whenever possible, to keep the mind fresh instead of getting bored.

When enough studying has been done that all the material that can be learned has been learned, and the test taker is prepared for the test, stop studying and do something relaxing such as listening to music, watching a movie, or taking a warm bubble bath.

There are also many other techniques to minimize the uneasiness or apprehension that is experienced along with test anxiety before, during, or even after the examination. In fact, there are a great deal of things that can be done to stop anxiety from interfering with lifestyle and performance. Again, remember that anxiety will not be eliminated entirely, and it shouldn't be. Otherwise that "up" feeling for exams would not exist, and most of us depend on that sensation to perform better than usual. However, this anxiety has to be at a level that is manageable.

Of course, as we have just discussed, being prepared for the exam is half the battle right away. Attending all classes, finding out what knowledge will be expected on the exam, and knowing the exam schedules are easy steps to lowering anxiety. Keeping up with work will remove the need to cram, and efficient study habits will eliminate wasted time. Studying should be done in an ideal location for concentration, so that it is simple to become interested in the material and give it complete attention. A method such as SQ3R (Survey, Question, Read, Recite, Review) is a wonderful key to follow to make sure that the study habits are as effective as possible, especially in the case of learning from a textbook. Flashcards are great techniques for memorization. Learning to take good notes will mean that notes will be full of useful information, so that less sifting will need to be done to seek out what is pertinent for studying. Reviewing notes after class and then again on occasion will keep the information fresh in the mind. From notes that have been taken summary sheets and outlines can be made for simpler reviewing.

A study group can also be a very motivational and helpful place to study, as there will be a sharing of ideas, all of the minds can work together, to make sure that everyone understands, and the studying will be made more interesting because it will be a social occasion.

Basically, though, as long as the test-taker remains organized and self confident, with efficient study habits, less time will need to be spent studying, and higher grades will be achieved.

To become self confident, there are many useful steps. The first of these is "self talk." It has been shown through extensive research, that self-talk for students who suffer from test anxiety, should be well monitored, in order to make sure that it contributes to self confidence as opposed to sinking the student. Frequently the self talk of test-anxious students is negative or self-defeating, thinking that everyone else is smarter and faster, that they always mess up, and that if they don't do well, they'll fail the entire course. It is important to decreasing anxiety that awareness is made of self talk. Try writing any negative self thoughts and then disputing them with a positive statement instead. Begin self-encouragement as though it was a friend speaking. Repeat positive statements to help reprogram the mind to believing in successes instead of failures.

Helpful Techniques

Other extremely helpful techniques include:

Self-visualization of doing well and reaching goals
While aiming for an "A" level of understanding, don't try to "overprotect" by setting your expectations lower. This will only convince the mind to stop studying in order to meet the lower expectations.
Don't make comparisons with the results or habits of other students. These are individual factors, and different things work for different people, causing different results.
Strive to become an expert in learning what works well, and what can be done in order to improve. Consider collecting this data in a journal.
Create rewards for after studying instead of doing things before studying that will only turn into avoidance behaviors.
Make a practice of relaxing - by using methods such as progressive relaxation, self-hypnosis, guided imagery, etc - in order to make relaxation an automatic sensation.
Work on creating a state of relaxed concentration so that concentrating will take on the focus of the mind, so that none will be wasted on worrying.
Take good care of the physical self by eating well and getting enough sleep.
Plan in time for exercise and stick to this plan.

Beyond these techniques, there are other methods to be used before, during and after the test that will help the test-taker perform well in addition to overcoming anxiety.

Before the exam comes the academic preparation. This involves establishing a study schedule and beginning at least one week before the actual date of the test. By doing this, the anxiety of not having enough time to study for the test will be automatically eliminated. Moreover, this will make the studying a much more effective experience, ensuring that the learning will be an easier process. This relieves much undue pressure on the test-taker.

Summary sheets, note cards, and flash cards with the main concepts and examples of these main concepts should be prepared in advance of the actual studying time. A topic should never be eliminated from this process. By omitting a topic because it isn't expected to be on the test is only setting up the test-taker for anxiety should it actually appear on the exam. Utilize the course syllabus for laying out the topics that should be studied. Carefully go over the notes that were made in class, paying special attention to any of the issues that the professor took special care to emphasize while lecturing in class. In the textbooks, use the chapter review, or if possible, the chapter tests, to begin your review.

It may even be possible to ask the instructor what information will be covered on the exam, or what the format of the exam will be (for example, multiple choice, essay, free form, true-false). Additionally, see if it is possible to find out how many questions will be on the test. If a review sheet or sample test has been offered by the professor, make good use of it, above anything else, for the preparation for the test. Another great resource for getting to know the examination is reviewing tests from previous semesters. Use these tests to review, and aim to achieve a 100% score on each of the possible topics. With a few exceptions, the goal that you set for yourself is the highest one that you will reach.

Take all of the questions that were assigned as homework, and rework them to any other possible course material. The more problems reworked, the more skill and confidence will form as a result. When forming the solution to a problem, write out each of the steps. Don't simply do head work. By doing as many steps on paper as possible, much clarification and therefore confidence will be formed. Do this with as many homework problems as possible, before checking the answers. By checking the answer after each problem, a reinforcement will exist, that will not be on the exam. Study situations should be as exam-like as possible, to prime the test-taker's system for the experience. By waiting to check the answers at the end, a psychological advantage will be formed, to decrease the stress factor.

Another fantastic reason for not cramming is the avoidance of confusion in concepts, especially when it comes to mathematics. 8-10 hours of study will become one hundred percent more effective if it is spread out over a week or at least several days, instead of doing it all in one sitting. Recognize that the human brain requires time in order to assimilate new material, so frequent breaks and a span of study time over several days will be much more beneficial.

Additionally, don't study right up until the point of the exam. Studying should stop a minimum of one hour before the exam begins. This allows the brain to rest and put things in their proper order. This will also provide the time to become as relaxed as possible when going into the examination room. The test-taker will also have time to eat well and eat sensibly. Know that the brain needs food as much as the rest of the body. With enough food and enough sleep, as well as a relaxed attitude, the body and the mind are primed for success.

Avoid any anxious classmates who are talking about the exam. These students only spread anxiety, and are not worth sharing the anxious sentimentalities.

Before the test also involves creating a positive attitude, so mental preparation should also be a point of concentration. There are many keys to creating a positive attitude. Should fears become rushing in, make a visualization of taking the exam, doing well, and seeing an A written on the paper. Write out a list of affirmations that will bring a feeling of confidence, such as "I am doing well in my English class," "I studied well and know my material," "I enjoy this class." Even if the affirmations aren't believed at first, it sends a positive message to the subconscious which will result in an alteration of the overall belief system, which is the system that creates reality.

If a sensation of panic begins, work with the fear and imagine the very worst! Work through the entire scenario of not passing the test, failing the entire course, and dropping out of school, followed by not getting a job, and pushing a shopping cart through the dark alley where you'll live. This will place things into perspective! Then, practice deep breathing and create a visualization of the opposite situation - achieving an "A" on the exam, passing the entire course, receiving the degree at a graduation ceremony.

On the day of the test, there are many things to be done to ensure the best results, as well as the most calm outlook. The following stages are suggested in order to maximize test-taking potential:

Begin the examination day with a moderate breakfast, and avoid any coffee or beverages with caffeine if the test taker is prone to jitters. Even people who are used to managing caffeine can feel jittery or light-headed when it is taken on a test day.
Attempt to do something that is relaxing before the examination begins. As last minute cramming clouds the mastering of overall concepts, it is better to use this time to create a calming outlook.
Be certain to arrive at the test location well in advance, in order to provide time to select a location that is away from doors, windows and other distractions, as well as giving enough time to relax before the test begins.
Keep away from anxiety generating classmates who will upset the sensation of stability and relaxation that is being attempted before the exam.

Should the waiting period before the exam begins cause anxiety, create a self-distraction by reading a light magazine or something else that is relaxing and simple.

During the exam itself, read the entire exam from beginning to end, and find out how much time should be allotted to each individual problem. Once writing the exam, should more time be taken for a problem, it should be abandoned, in order to begin another problem. If there is time at the end, the unfinished problem can always be returned to and completed.

Read the instructions very carefully - twice - so that unpleasant surprises won't follow during or after the exam has ended.

When writing the exam, pretend that the situation is actually simply the completion of homework within a library, or at home. This will assist in forming a relaxed atmosphere, and will allow the brain extra focus for the complex thinking function.

Begin the exam with all of the questions with which the most confidence is felt. This will build the confidence level regarding the entire exam and will begin a quality momentum. This will also create encouragement for trying the problems where uncertainty resides.

Going with the "gut instinct" is always the way to go when solving a problem. Second guessing should be avoided at all costs. Have confidence in the ability to do well.

For essay questions, create an outline in advance that will keep the mind organized and make certain that all of the points are remembered. For multiple choice, read every answer, even if the correct one has been spotted - a better one may exist.

Continue at a pace that is reasonable and not rushed, in order to be able to work carefully. Provide enough time to go over the answers at the end, to check for small errors that can be corrected.

Should a feeling of panic begin, breathe deeply, and think of the feeling of the body releasing sand through its pores. Visualize a calm, peaceful place, and include all of the sights, sounds and sensations of this image. Continue the deep breathing, and take a few minutes to continue this with closed eyes. When all is well again, return to the test.

If a "blanking" occurs for a certain question, skip it and move on to the next question. There will be time to return to the other question later. Get everything done that can be done, first, to guarantee all the grades that can be compiled, and to build all of the confidence possible. Then return to the weaker questions to build the marks from there.

Remember, one's own reality can be created, so as long as the belief is there, success will follow. And remember: anxiety can happen later, right now, there's an exam to be written!

After the examination is complete, whether there is a feeling for a good grade or a bad grade, don't dwell on the exam, and be certain to follow through on the reward that was promised...and enjoy it! Don't dwell on any mistakes that have been made, as there is nothing that can be done at this point anyway.

Additionally, don't begin to study for the next test right away. Do something relaxing for a while, and let the mind relax and prepare itself to begin absorbing information again.

From the results of the exam - both the grade and the entire experience, be certain to learn from what has gone on. Perfect studying habits and work some more on confidence in order to make the next examination experience even better than the last one.
Learn to avoid places where openings occurred for laziness, procrastination and day dreaming.

Use the time between this exam and the next one to better learn to relax, even learning to relax on cue, so that any anxiety can be controlled during the next exam. Learn how to relax the body. Slouch in your chair if that helps. Tighten and then relax all of the different muscle groups, one group at a time, beginning with the feet and then working all the way up to the neck and face. This will ultimately relax the muscles more than they were to begin with. Learn how to breathe deeply and comfortably, and focus on this breathing going in and out as a relaxing thought. With every exhale, repeat the word "relax."

As common as test anxiety is, it is very possible to overcome it. Make yourself one of the test-takers who overcome this frustrating hindrance.

Special Report: Retaking the Test: What Are Your Chances at Improving Your Score?

After going through the experience of taking a major test, many test takers feel that once is enough. The test usually comes during a period of transition in the test taker's life, and taking the test is only one of a series of important events. With so many distractions and conflicting recommendations, it may be difficult for a test taker to rationally determine whether or not he should retake the test after viewing his scores.

The importance of the test usually only adds to the burden of the retake decision. However, don't be swayed by emotion. There a few simple questions that you can ask yourself to guide you as you try to determine whether a retake would improve your score:

1. What went wrong? Why wasn't your score what you expected?

Can you point to a single factor or problem that you feel caused the low score? Were you sick on test day? Was there an emotional upheaval in your life that caused a distraction? Were you late for the test or not able to use the full time allotment? If you can point to any of these specific, individual problems, then a retake should definitely be considered.

2. Is there enough time to improve?

Many problems that may show up in your score report may take a lot of time for improvement. A deficiency in a particular math skill may require weeks or months of tutoring and studying to improve. If you have enough time to improve an identified weakness, then a retake should definitely be considered.

3. How will additional scores be used? Will a score average, highest score, or most recent score be used?

Different test scores may be handled completely differently. If you've taken the test multiple times, sometimes your highest score is used, sometimes your average score is computed and used, and sometimes your most recent score is used. Make sure you understand what method will be used to evaluate your scores, and use that to help you determine whether a retake should be considered.

4. Are my practice test scores significantly higher than my actual test score?

If you have taken a lot of practice tests and are consistently scoring at a much higher level than your actual test score, then you should consider a retake. However, if you've taken five practice tests and only one of your scores was higher than your actual test score, or if your practice test scores were only slightly higher than your actual test score, then it is unlikely that you will significantly increase your score.

5. Do I need perfect scores or will I be able to live with this score? Will this score still allow me to follow my dreams?

What kind of score is acceptable to you? Is your current score "good enough?" Do you have to have a certain score in order to pursue the future of your dreams? If you won't be happy with your current score, and there's no way that you could live with it, then you should consider a retake. However, don't get your hopes up. If you are looking for significant improvement, that may or may not be possible. But if you won't be happy otherwise, it is at least worth the effort.

Remember that there are other considerations. To achieve your dream, it is likely that your grades may also be taken into account. A great test score is usually not the only thing necessary to succeed. Make sure that you aren't overemphasizing the importance of a high test score.

Furthermore, a retake does not always result in a higher score. Some test takers will score lower on a retake, rather than higher. One study shows that one-fourth of test takers will achieve a significant improvement in test score, while one-sixth of test takers will actually show a decrease. While this shows that most test takers will improve, the majority will only improve their scores a little and a retake may not be worth the test taker's effort.

Finally, if a test is taken only once and is considered in the added context of good grades on the part of a test taker, the person reviewing the grades and scores may be tempted to assume that the test taker just had a bad day while taking the test, and may discount the low test score in favor of the high grades. But if the test is retaken and the scores are approximately the same, then the validity of the low scores are only confirmed. Therefore, a retake could actually hurt a test taker by definitely bracketing a test taker's score ability to a limited range.

Additional Bonus Material

Due to our efforts to try to keep this book to a manageable length, we've created a link that will give you access to all of your additional bonus material.

Please visit http://www.mometrix.com/bonus948/accuplacermath to access the information.